THE SUPREME SIGN

Observations of a Traveller Questioning Creation Concerning his Maker

by
BEDIUZZAMAN SAID NURSI

A PUBLICATION OF
RISALE-I NUR INSTITUTE OF AMERICA

Sixth in a series of translations published by the Risale-i Nur Institute of America.

Translated from the Turkish and Arabic
by Hamid Algar, Professor of Near Eastern Studies at the University of California, Berkeley, California, U.S.A.

Library of Congress
Catalog Card Number: 79-65614

ISBN 0-933552-08-4

PRINTED IN THE UNITED STATES OF AMERICA at Golden Horn Typesetting & Publishing House, 1301 University Avenue, Berkeley, California 94702.

Contents

Statement of Purpose   7

Introduction   10

First Chapter   19

Second Chapter   94

Question and Answer   146

The Seed of Paradise   155

A Comparison   167

Extract from a Letter   181

A Defense Speech   185

An important warning
and statement of purpose

Not everyone will be able to understand all the matters discussed in this most significant book, but equally nobody will remain portionless. If somebody enters a garden, he will find that his hands cannot reach all the fruit it contains, but the amount that falls within his grasp will be enough for him. The garden does not exist for him alone; it exists also for those whose arms are longer than his.

There are five causes making difficult the understanding of this book.

The first: I have written down my own observations, according to my own understanding, and for myself. I have not written according to the understanding and conceptions of others, as is the case with other books.

The second: since the reality of divine unity is set forth in this book, in the most comprehensive form, by virtue of a manifestation of the Supreme Name, the subjects discussed are extremely broad, extremely profound and sometimes extremely long. Not everyone can comprehend these matters all at once.

7

The third: since each matter constitutes a great and extensive truth, a single sentence will sometimes stretch out over a whole page or more, in order not to fracture the truth in question. A single proof requires copious preliminaries.

The fourth: since most of the matters contained in the book have numerous proofs and evidences, the discussion sometimes becomes prolix through the inclusion of ten or twenty proofs by way of demonstration. Limited intelligences cannot understand this.

The fifth: it is true that I received the manifestation of the lights of this book from the effulgence of Ramadan. Nonetheless, I was distraught in a number of respects, and I wrote the book hastily at a time my body was wracked by several illnesses, without revising the first draft. I felt, moreover, that I was not writing with my own will and volition, and it seemed inappropriate to rearrange or correct what I had written, according to my own thoughts. This, too, resulted in rendering the book difficult of comprehension. In addition, a number of sections in Arabic crept in, and the First Station, written entirely in Arabic, was removed from the book and made into a separate work.

Despite the defects and difficulties arising from these five causes, this treatise has such an importance that Imam Ali — may God be pleased with him — miraculously foresaw its composition and gave it the names "Supreme Sign" and "Staff of Moses." He looked upon this part of the *Risale-i Nur* with special favor, and directed men's gazes toward it.* The Supreme Sign is a true exposition of the Supreme Verse,** and it constitutes at the same time the Seventh Ray, designated by the Imam as the Staff of Moses.

This treatise consists of an introduction and two chapters. The introduction sets forth four important matters; the First Chapter contains the Arabic portion of the exposition of the Supreme Verse; and the Second Chapter consists of the translation of that exposition together with the accompanying proofs.

Too much has been explained in the following introduction, but it was not my intention to lengthen it thus. The fact that it was written at this length indicates the existence of a need. Indeed, some people may regard it as too short, despite its length.

—Said Nursi

---

*The events that took place in Denizli fully confirmed the prediction of Imam Ali concerning the Supreme Sign. For the secret printing of this book was the cause of our imprisonment, and the majesty of its sacred and most powerful truth was the main cause of our acquittal and deliverance. Thus did Imam Ali make manifest his miraculous prediction, and prove the acceptance of the prayer he had uttered on our behalf: "by means of the Supreme Sign, secure me against sudden death!"

**See footnote (1) on page 10.

Introduction

"I created not jinn and mankind except that they might worship Me!"[1]

By virtue of the mystery of this mighty verse, the purpose for the sending of man to this world and the wisdom implicit in it, consists of knowing the Creator of all beings or believing in Him and worshipping Him. The primordial duty of man and the obligation incumbent upon him are to know God and believe in Him, to assent to His Being and Unity in submission and perfect certainty.

For man, who by nature desires permanent life and immortal existence, whose unlimited hopes are matched by boundless afflictions, any object or accomplishment other than faith in God, knowledge of God and the means for attaining these which are the fundament and key of eternal life — any such object or accomplishment must be regarded as lowly for man, or even worthless in many cases.

Since this truth has been proven with firm evidence in the *Risale-i Nur* (Treatise of Light), we

1. Qur'an 51:56

10

refer exposition of it to that Treatise, setting forth here, within the framework of four questions, only two abysses that shake certainty of faith in this age and induce hesitation.

The means for salvation from the first abyss are these two questions.

The first question: As proven in detail in the Thirteenth Flash of the Thirty-First Letter, in general questions denial has no value in the face of proof and is extremely weak. For example, with respect to the sighting of the crescent moon at the beginning of Ramadan the Noble, if two common men prove the crescent to have emerged by their witnessing it, and thousands of nobles and scholars deny it, saying "we have not seen it," their negation is valueless and without power to convince. When it is a question of proof each person strengthens and supports the other, and consensus results. But when it is a question of negation, there is no difference between one man and a thousand. Each person remains alone and isolated. For the one who affirms looks beyond himself and judges the matter as it is. Thus in the example we have given if one says "the moon is in the sky," and his friend then points his finger at the moon, the two of them unite and are strengthened.

The one who engages in negation and denial, however, does not regard the matter as it is, and is even unable to do so. For it is a well-known principle that "a non-particularized denial, not directed to a particular locus, cannot be proven."

For example, if I affirm the existence of a thing

in the world, and you deny it, I can easily establish
its existence with a single indication. But for you
to justify your negation, that is to establish the
non-existence of the thing — it is necessary to
hunt exhaustively through the whole world, and
even to examine every aspect of past ages. Only
then can you say, "it does not exist, and never
has existed."

Since those who negate and deny do not regard
the matter as it is but judge rather in the light
of their own souls, and their own intelligence
and vision, they can in no way strengthen and
support each other. For the veils and causes that
prevent them from seeing and knowing are various.
Anyone can say, "I do not see it; therefore,
in my opinion and belief, it does not exist." But
none can say, "it does not exist in actuality."
If someone says this — particularly in questions
of faith touching on all beings — it is a lie as
vast as the world itself, and he who utters it
will be incapable both of speaking the truth and
of being corrected.

In short, the result is one and single in the
case of affirmation, and every instance of affirmation supports all other instances.

Negation by contrast is not one, but multiple.
Multiplicity arises through each person's saying
concerning himself, "in my opinion and view,"
or "in my belief," and leads to multiplicity of
result. Hence each separate instance cannot support all other instances.

Therefore with respect to the truth with which
we began, there is no significance in the multip-

licity and apparent predominance of the un-believers and deniers who oppose belief. Now it is necessary to refrain from introducing any hesitation into the certainty and faith of a believer, but in this age the negations and denials of the philosophers of Europe have induced doubt in a number of unfortunate dupes and thus destroyed their certainty and obliterated their eternal felicity. Death and the coming of one's appointed hour, which afflict thirty thousand men each day, are deprived of their meaning of dismissal from this world and presented as eternal annihilation. The grave with its ever-open door, constantly threatens the denier with annihilation and poisons his life with the bitterest of sorrows. Appreciate then how great a blessing is faith, and the very essence of life.

The second question: with respect to a problem subject to discussion in an art or a trade, those who stand outside that art or trade cannot speak authoritatively, however great, learned and accomplished they may be, nor can their judgements be accepted as decisive. They cannot form part of the learned consensus of the art.

For example, the judgement of a great engineer on the diagnosis and cure of a disease does not have the same value as that of the lowliest physician. In particular, the words of denial of a philosopher who is absorbed in the material sphere, who becomes continually more remote from the spiritual and cruder and more insensitive to light, whose intelligence is restricted to what his eye beholds — the words of such a one are unworthy of consideration and valueless with respect to spiritual matters.

On matters sacred and spiritual and concerning the divine unity, there is total accord among the hundreds of thousands of the People of Truth, such as Shaykh Gilani — may his mystery be sanctified! — who beheld God's Supreme throne while still on the earth, who spent ninety years advancing in spiritual work, and who had unveiled to him the verities of the faith in all three stations of certainty. This being the case what value have the words of philosophers, who through their absorption in the most diffuse details of the material realm and the most minute aspects of multiplicity are choking and dazed? Are not their denials and objections drowned out like the buzzing of a fly by the roaring of thunder?

The essence of the unbelief that opposes the truths of Islam and struggles against them is denial, ignorance, and negation. Even though in outer form it may appear to be an affirmation of some kind, and a manifestation of being, it is in reality negation and non-being. Whereas faith is knowledge and a manifestation of being; it is affirmation and judgement. Even a negating aspect of religion is the gate to a positive truth or the veil covering it. If the unbelievers who struggle against faith attempt, with the utmost difficulty, to affirm and accept their negative beliefs in the form of acceptance and admission of non-being, then their unbelief may be regarded as a form of knowledge or judgement mistaken and erroneous in one respect. But as for non-acceptance, denial and non-admission — something more easily done — it is absolute ignorance and total absence of judgement.

The convictions underlying unbelief are then of two kinds.

The first pays no regard to the truths of Islam. It is an erroneous admission, a baseless belief and a mistaken acceptance peculiar to itself; it is an unjust judgement. This kind of unbelief is beyond the scope of our discussion. It has no concern with us, nor do we have any concern with it.

The second kind opposes the verities of the faith and struggles against them. It consists in turn of two varieties.

The first is non-acceptance. It consists simply of not consenting to affirmation. This is a species of ignorance; there is no judgement involved and it occurs easily. It too is beyond the scope of our discussion.

The second variety is acceptance of non-being. It is to consent to non-being with one's heart, and a judgement is involved. It is a conviction and something stable with its own consistency. It is on account of this consistency that it is obliged to affirm its negation.

This negation comprises two types:

The first type says: "a certain thing does not exist at a certain place or in a particular direction." This kind of denial can be proved, and it lies outside of our discussion.

The second type consists of negating and denying

those doctrinal and sacred matters, general and comprehensive, that concern this world, creation, the hereafter, and the succession of different ages. This kind of negation cannot in any fashion be substantiated, as we have shown in the first question, for what is needed to substantiate such negations is a vision that shall encompass all of creation, behold the hereafter and observe every aspect of time without limit.

The second abyss and the means for escaping it: This too consists of two matters.

The first: Intelligences that become narrowed by absorption in neglect of God and in sin, or the material realm, when confronted with magnificence, splendor and infinity, are unable to comprehend lofty matters; hence taking pride in such knowledge as they have, they hasten to denial and negation. Since they cannot encompass the extremely vast, profound and comprehensive questions of faith within their straitened and dessicated intellects, their corrupt and spiritually moribund hearts, they cast themselves into unbelief and misguidance, and choke.

If they were able to look at the true nature of their unbelief and the essence of their misguidance they would see that, compared to the reasonable, suitable and indeed necessary awe that is present in faith, their unbelief conceals and contains manifold absurdity and impossibility. The *Risale-i Nur* (Treatise of Light) has proven this truth by hundreds of comparisons with the same finality that "two plus two equals four." For example, one who does not accept the neces-

sary Being, the eternity and the comprehensiveness
of attribute of God Almighty, on account of
their awesomeness, may form a creed of unbelief
by assigning that necessary being, eternity and
comprehensiveness of attribute to an unlimited
number of creatures, an infinity of atoms. Or
like the foolish sophists, he can abdicate his
intelligence by denying and negating both his
own being and that of all creatures.

Thus, all the truths of faith and Islam, drawing
upon the awesomeness that is required by their
nature and dignity, deliver themselves from the
horrendous absurdities, the terrifying superstitions
and the tenebrous ignorance of unbelief that
confront them, and take up their place in sound
hearts and straight intellects, through utmost
submission and assent.

The constant proclamation of this awesomeness
and might in the call to prayer, in the prayer
itself and in most of the rites of Islam,

Allahuakbar[2], Allahuakbar,
Allahuakbar, Allahuakbar;

the declaration of the Sacred Tradition that "awesomeness is My shield, and splendor is My cloak;"
and the statement of the Prophet — peace and
blessings be upon him — his most inspiring com-
muning with God, in the eighty-sixth part of *Jaushan al-Kabir*:* 'O Thou other than Whose Kingdom no kingdom exists; o Thou Whose praise can-

2. Allah is the Most Great.

*An important prayer book compiled and edited by the
author.

not be counted by His slaves; o Thou Whose Glory cannot be described by His creatures; o Thou Whose Perfection lies beyond the range of all vision; o Thou Whose Attributes exceed the bounds of all understanding; o Thou Whose Magnificence is beyond the reach of all thought; o Thou Whose Qualities man cannot fittingly describe; o Thou Whose decree His slaves cannot avert; o Thou Whose Signs are manifest — be Thou glorified; there is no god other than Thee — protection, protection, deliver us from the fire': all of these show that awesomeness and magnificence constitute a necessary veil.

★ ★ ★

The Supreme Sign

The observations of a traveller
questioning creation concerning his maker

FIRST CHAPTER

(Concerning the proofs of Necessary Existence)

> In the Name of God, the Compassionate,
> the Merciful.
> All that is in the seven heavens and the earth
> glorifies Him with praise, but ye understand
> not their glorifying — He is Most Fore-
> bearing, Most Pardoning![3]

This second station, in addition to explaining
this sublime verse, also sets out the proofs and
evidences of the foregoing first station, one written
in Arabic but here translated.

Since this sublime verse, like many other Qur'-
anic verses, mentions first the heavens — that
brilliant page proclaiming God's unity, gazed on
at all times and by all men with wonder and joy
— in its pronouncement of the creator of this
cosmos, let us, too, begin with a mention of
the heavens.

Indeed, every voyager who comes to the hospice
and the realm of this world, opens his eyes and

3. Qur'an 17:44

wonders who is the master of this fine hospice, which resembles a most generous banquet, a most ingenious exhibition, a most impressive camp and training ground, a most amazing and wondrous place of recreation, a most profound and wise place of instruction. He asks himself too who is the author of this great book, and who is the monarch of this lofty realm. There first presents itself to him the beautiful face of the heavens, inscribed with the gilt lettering of the stars. That face calls him saying, "Look at me, and I shall guide you to what you seek." He looks then and sees a manifestation of dominicality performing various tasks in the heavens: it holds aloft in the heavens, without any supporting pillar, hundreds of thousands of heavenly bodies, some of which are a thousand times heavier than the earth and revolve seventy times faster than a cannonball; it causes them to move in harmony and swiftly without colliding with each other; it causes innumerable lamps to burn constantly, without the use of any oil; it disposes of these great masses without any disturbance or disorder; it sets sun and moon to work at their respective tasks, without those great bodies ever rebelling; it administers within an infinite space — one that cannot be comprehended in figures and is marked out by two poles — all that exists, at the same time, with the same strength, in the same fashion, manner and mould, without the least deficiency; it reduces to submissive obedience to its law all the aggressive powers inherent in those bodies; it cleanses and lustrates the face of the heavens, removing all the sweepings and refuse of that vast assembly; it causes those bodies to maneuvre like a disciplined army; and then, making the earth revolve, it shows the heavens each night and each year in a different form, like a cinema screen displaying true and imaginative scenes to the audience of creation. There is within this dominical activity a truth consisting of subjugation, administration, revolution, ordering, cleansing and commanding. This truth, with its sublimity and comprehensiveness, bears witness to the Necessary Existence and Unity of the Creator of the Heavens and testifies to that Existence being more manifest than that of the Heavens. Hence it was said in the First Step of the First Station:

"There is no god but God, the Necessary Being, to Whose Necessary existence in Unity the Heavens and all they contain testify, through the testimony of the sublimity of the comprehensiveness of the truth of subjugation, administration, revolution, ordering, cleansing and commanding, a truth vast and completed by observation."

★ ★ ★

THEN THAT WONDROUS place of gathering known as space or the atmosphere begins thunderously to proclaim to that traveller come as a guest to the world, "Look at me! You can discover and find through me the object of your search, the one who sent you here!'' The traveller looks at the sour but kind face of the atmosphere, and listening to the awesome but joyous thunderclaps perceives the following.

The clouds, suspended between the sky and the earth, water the garden of the world in the most wise and merciful fashion, furnish the inhabitants of the earth with the Water of Life, modify the natural heat of life, and hasten to bestow aid wherever it is needed. In addition to fulfilling these and other duties, the vast clouds, capable of filling the heavens, sometimes hide themselves, with their parts retiring to rest so that not a trace can be seen, just like a well disciplined army showing and hiding itself in accordance with sudden orders.

Then, the very instant that the command is given to pour down rain, the clouds gather in one hour, or rather in a few minutes; they fill the sky and await further orders from their commander.

Next the traveller looks at the wind in the atmosphere and sees that the air is employed wisely and generously in such numerous tasks that it is as if each of the inanimate atoms of that unconscious air were hearing and noting the orders coming from the Commander of All Being; without neglecting a single one of them, it performs them in ordered fashion and through the power of that commander. Thereby it gives breath to all beings and conveys to all living things the heat, light and electricity they need, as well as aiding in the pollination of plants. All these general functions and services show that it is being employed, in the most conscious, wise and life-giving fashion, by an unseen hand.

The traveller then looks at the rain and sees that within those delicate, glistening sweet drops, sent from a hidden treasury of mercy, there are so many compassionate gifts and functions contained that it is as if mercy itself were assuming shape and flowing forth from the divine treasury in the form of drops. It is for this reason that rain has been called "mercy."

Next the traveller looks at the lightning and listens to the thunder and sees that both of these, too, are employed in wondrous tasks.

Then he looks inward and examining his intellect says: "the inanimate, lifeless cloud that resembles carded cotton has of course no knowledge of us; when it comes to our aid, it is not because it takes pity on us. It cannot appear and disappear without receiving orders. Rather it acts in accordance with the orders of a most Powerful and Merciful Commander. First it disappears without leaving a trace, then suddenly reappears in order to begin its work. By the command and power of a most active and exalted, a most Magnificent and Splendid Monarch, it fills and then empties the atmosphere. Inscribing the sky with wisdom and erasing the pattern, it makes of the sky a tablet of effacement and affirmation, a depiction of the gathering and the resurrection. By the contriving of a most Generous and Bountiful, a most Munificent and

Solicitous Lord, it mounts the wind and taking with it treasuries of rain each as heavy as a mountain, hastens to the aid of the needy. It is as if it were weeping over them in pity, with its tears causing the flowers to smile, tempering the heat of the sun, spraying gardens with water, and washing and cleansing the face of the earth."

That wondering traveller then tells his own intellect: "These hundreds of thousands of wise, merciful and ingenious tasks and acts of generosity and mercy that arise from the veil and outer form of this inanimate, lifeless, unconscious, volatile, unstable, stormy, unsettled and inconstant air, clearly establish that this diligent wind, this tireless servant, never acts of itself, but rather in accordance with the orders of a most Wise and Generous commander. It is as if each particle were aware of every single task, like a soldier understanding and hearkening to every order of its commander, for it hears and obeys every divine command that courses through the air. It aids all animals to breathe and to live, all plants to pollinate and grow, and cultivates all the matter necessary for their survival. It directs and administers the clouds, makes possible the voyaging of sailing ships, and enables sounds to be conveyed, particularly by means of wireless, telephone, telegraph and radio, as well as numerous other universal functions. Now these atoms, each composed of two such simple materials as hydrogen and oxygen and each resembling the other, exist in hundreds of thousands of different fashions all over the globe; I conclude therefore that they are being employed and set to work in the utmost orderliness by a Hidden Hand.''

''As the verse makes clear,

> 'and the disposition of the winds and the clouds, held in disciplined order between the heavens and the earth,⁴'

the one who through the disposition of the winds employs them in countless divine functions, who through the ordering of the winds uses them in infinite tasks of mercy, and who creates the air in this fashion — such a one can only be the Possessor of Necessary Existence, the One Empowered over All Things and Knowledgeable of All Things, the Lord Endowed with Splendor and Generosity.'' This is the conclusion our traveller now draws.

Then he looks at the rain and sees that within it are contained benefits as numerous as the raindrops, and divine manifestations as multiple as the particles of rain, and instances of providential wisdom as plentiful as its atoms. Those sweet, delicate and blessed drops are moreover created in so beautiful and ordered a fashion, that particularly the rain sent in the summertime, is dispatched and caused to fall with such balance and regularity that not even stormy winds that cause large objects to collide can destroy its equilibrium and order; the drops do not collide with each other or merge in such fashion as to become harmful masses of water. Water,

4. Qur'an 2:164

composed of two simple elements like hydrogen and oxygen, is employed in hundred of thousands of other wise, purposeful tasks and arts, particularly in animate beings; although it is itself inanimate and unconscious. Rain which is then mercy embodied in form can only be manufactured in the unseen treasury of the One Compassionate and Merciful; its descent on the earth is like a commentary on the verse,

"and He it is Who sends down rain after men have despaired, and thus spreads out His Mercy. [5]"

The traveller next listens to the thunder and watches the lightning. He understands that these two wondrous celestial events are like a material demonstration of the verses,

"the thunder glorifies His praise,[6]"

"the brilliance of His lightning almost robs them of their sight.[7]"

They also announce the coming of rain, and thus give glad tidings to the needy.

Yes, this sudden utterance of a miraculous sound by the heavens; the filling of the dark sky with the flash and fire of lightning; the setting alight of the clouds that resemble mountains

5. Qur'an 42:28
6. Qur'an 13:13
7. Qur'an 24:43

of cotton or pipes bursting with water and snow — these and similar phenomena are like a blow struck on the head of the negligent man whose gaze is directed down at the earth. They tell him:

"Lift up your head, look at the miraculous deeds of the most active and powerful being who wishes to make himself known. In the same way that you are not left to your own devices, so too, these phenomena and events have a master and purpose. Each of them is caused to fulfil a particular task, and each is employed by a Most Wise Disposer of all things."

The wondering traveller hears then the lofty and manifest testimony to the truth that is composed of the disposition of the winds, the descent of the rains and the administration of the heavens, and says "I believe in God." That which was stated in the second stage of the First Station expresses the observations of the traveller concerning space and the heavens:

"There is no god but God, the Necessary Being, to Whose Necessary Existence in Unity the heavens and all they contain testify, through the testimony of the sublimity of the comprehensiveness of the truth of subjugation, administration, revolution, ordering, cleansing and commanding, a truth vast and completed by observation."

★ ★ ★

NEXT, THE GLOBE addresses that thoughtful travel-ler, now growing accustomed to his reflective journey:

"Why are you wandering through the heavens, through space and the sky? Come, I will make known to you what you are seeking. Look at the functions that I perform and read my pages!" He looks and sees that the globe, like an ecstatic Mevlevi dervish with its twofold motion, is tracing out around the field of the Supreme Gathering a circle that determines the succession of days, years and seasons. It is a most magnifi-cent divine ship, loaded with the hundreds of thousands of different forms of food and equip-ment needed for all animate beings, floating with the utmost equilibrium in the ocean of space and circling the sun.

He then looks at the pages of the earth and sees that each page of each of its chapters proc-laims the Lord of the Earth in thousands of verses. Being unable to read the whole of it, he looks at the page dealing with the creation and deploy-ment of animate beings in the spring, and ob-serves the following:

The forms of the countless members of hund-reds of thousands of species emerge, in the utmost precision, from a simple material and are then nurtured in most merciful fashion. Then, in mirac-ulous manner, wings are given to some of the seeds; they take to flight, and are thus dispersed. They are most effectively distributed, most care-fully fed and nurtured. Countless tasty and delicious forms of food, in the most merciful and tender fashion, are brought forth from dry clay, and from roots, seeds and drops of liquid that differ little among each other. Every spring, a hundred thousand kinds of food and equipment are loaded on, as if to a railway wagon, and are dispatched in utmost orderliness to animate beings. The sending to infants of canned milk in those food packages, and pumps of sugared milk in the form of their mothers' affectionate breasts, is in particular such an instance of solicitousness, mercy and wisdom that it immediately establishes itself as a most tender manifestation of the mercy and generosity of the Merciful and Compassionate One.

In sum, the page of vernal life displays a hundred thousand examples and samples of the Supreme Gathering, and is a tangible demonstration of this verse,

> "so look to the signs of God's mercy: how He gives life to the earth after its death, for verily He it is Who gives life to the dead, and He is empowered over all things.[8]"

Conversely, this verse may be said to express in miraculous fashion the meanings of the page that is the spring. The traveller thus understood that the earth proclaims on all its pages, in a fashion appropriate to their size:

> "there is no god but He."[9]

8. Qur'an 30:50
9. A phrase repeated many times in Qur'an.

In expression of the meaning beheld by the traveller through the brief testimony of one of the twenty aspects of a single page out of the more than twenty pages of the globe, it was said in the Third Step of the First Station:

"There is no god but God, the Necessary Being, to Whose Necessary Existence in Unity the earth with all that is in it and upon it testifies, through the testimony of the sublimity of the comprehensiveness of the truth of subjugation, disposition, nurturing, opening, distribution of seeds, protection, administration, the giving of life to all animate beings, compassion and mercy universal and general, a truth vast and completed by observation."

★ ★ ★

THEN THAT reflective traveller read each page of the cosmos, and as he did so his faith, that key to felicity, strengthened; his gnosis, that key to spiritual progress, increased; his belief in God, the source and foundation of all perfection, developed one degree more; his joy and pleasure augmented and aroused his eagerness; and while listening to the perfect and convincing lessons given by the sky, by space and the earth, he cried out for more. Then he heard the rapturous invocation of God made by the tumult of the seas and the great rivers, and listened to their sad yet pleasant sounds. In numerous ways they were saying to him: "Look at us, read also our signs!" Looking, our traveller saw the following:

The seas, constantly and vitally surging, merging and pouring forth with an inclination to conquest inherent in their very nature, surrounded the earth, and together with the earth, revolved, extremely swiftly, in a circle of twenty-five thousand years in a single year. Yet the seas did not disperse, did not overflow or encroach on the land contiguous to them. They moved and stood still, and were protected by the command and power of a most powerful and magnificent being.

Then looking to the depths of the sea, the traveller saw that apart from the most beautiful, well-adorned and symmetrical jewels, there were thousands of different kinds of animal, sustained and ordered, brought to life and caused to die, in so disciplined a fashion, their provision coming from mere sand and salt water, that it established irresistibly the existence of a Powerful and Glorious, a Merciful and Beauteous Being administering and giving life to them.

The traveller then looks at the rivers and sees that the benefits inherent in them, the functions they perform, and their continual replenishment, are inspired by such wisdom and mercy as indisputably to prove that all rivers, springs, streams and great waterways flow forth from the treasury of Mercy of the Compassionate One, the Lord of Splendor and Generosity. They are preserved and dispensed, indeed, in so extraordinary a fashion that it is said "four rivers flow forth from Paradise."That is, they transcend by far external causality, and flow forth instead from the treasury of a non-material Paradise, from the superabundance of an unseen and inexhaustible source.

For example, the blessed Nile, that turns the sandy land of Egypt into a paradise, flows from the Mountains of the Moon in the south without ever being exhausted, as if it were a small sea. If the water that flowed down the river in six months were gathered together in the form of a mountain and then frozen, it would be larger than those mountains. But the place in the mountains where the water is lodged and stored is less than a sixth of their mass. As for the water that replenishes the river, the rain that enters the reservoir of the river is very sparse in that torrid region and is quickly swallowed up by the thirsty soil; hence it is incapable of maintaining the equilibrium of the river. A tradition has thus grown up that the blessed Nile springs, in miraculous fashion, from an unseen paradise. This tradition has profound meaning and expresses a beautiful truth.

The traveller saw, then, a thousandth part of the truths and affirmations contained in the oceans and rivers. The seas proclaim unanimously with a power proportionate to their extent, "there is no god but He," and produce as witnesses to their testimony all the creatures that inhabit them. This, our traveller perceived.

Expressing and conveying the testimony of the seas and the rivers, we said, in the Fourth Step of the First Station:

"There is no god but God, the Necessary Existent, to the necessity of Whose Existence in Unity point all the seas and the rivers, together with all they contain, by the testimony of the magnificence of the comprehensiveness of the truth of subjugation, preservation, and dispensation, vast and orderly."

★ ★ ★

THEN THE TRAVELLER is summoned, on his meditative journey, by the mountains and the plains. "Read too our pages," they say. Looking he sees that the universal function and duty of mountains is of such splendor and wisdom as to stupefy the intelligence. The mountains emerge from the earth by the command of their Lord, thereby palliating the turmoil, anger and rancor that arise from disturbances within the earth. As the mountains surge upward, the earth begins to breathe; it is delivered from harmful tremors and upheavals, and its tranquility as it pursues its duty of rotation is no longer disturbed. In the same way that masts are planted in ships to preserve them from turbulence, so too mountains are set up on the deck of the ship that is the earth, as is indicated by verses of the Qur'an of Miraculous Exposition such as these:

"and the mountains as pegs[10],"

10. Qur'an 78:7

"and We have cast down anchors[11],"
"and the mountains He anchored them[12],"

Then, too, there are stored up and preserved in the mountains all kinds of springs, waters, minerals and other materials needed by animate beings, in so wise, skillful, generous and foreseeing a fashion that they prove the existence of the storehouses and warehouses of One of Infinite Power and Infinite Wisdom. The traveller thus sees the universal wisdom inherent in the mountains and plains — wisdom which he deduces to exist in other things too — and the fashion in which all manner of things are stored up in them, to be like a declaration of God's unity, a declaration as powerful and firm as the mountains and vast and expansive as the plains. So he too says, "I believe in God."

In expression of this meaning, it was said in the Fifth Step of the First Station:

"There is no god but God, to the necessity of Whose Existence point all the mountains and plains together with what is in them and upon them, by the testimony of the magnificence of the comprehensiveness of the truth of the preservation, administration, dissemination of seed and dispensation, dominical, vast, universal, disciplined, orderly and perfect."

★ ★ ★

11. Qur'an 50:7
12. Qur'an 79:32

THEN, WHILE THAT traveller was travelling in his mind through the mountains and plains, the gate to the arboreal and vegetable realm was opened before him. He was summoned inside: "come," they said, "inspect our realm and read our inscriptions." Entering, he saw that a splendid and well-adorned assembly for the proclamation of God's power and unity, a circle to invoke Him and offer Him thanks, had been drawn up. He understood from the very appearance of all trees and plants that their different species were proclaiming unanimously, "there is no god but God." For he perceived three great and general truths indicating and proving that all fruit-giving trees and plants with the tongue of their symmetrical and eloquent leaves, the phrases of their charming and loquacious flowers, the words of their well-ordered and well-spoken fruits, were testifying to God's glory and bearing witness that "there is no god but He."

The first of those truths: in the same way that in each of the plants and trees a deliberate bounty and generosity is to be seen in most obvious fashion, and a purposive liberality and munificence, so too it is to be seen in the totality of the trees and plants, with the brilliance of sunlight.

The second: the wise and purposive distinction and differentiation among the different species, one that cannot in any way be attributed to chance, the deliberate and merciful adornment and illustration that is inherent in them — all this is to be seen as clearly as daylight in the infinite varieties and species; they show themselves to be the work and the imprint of an All-Wise Maker.

The third: the opening and blossoming of all the separate members of the hundred thousand species of that infinite realm, each in its own distinct fashion and shape, in the utmost order, equilibrium and beauty, from well-defined and limited, simple and solid, seeds and grains, identical to each other or nearly so — their emerging from those seeds in distinct and separate form, with utter equilibrium, vitality and wise purpose without the least error or mistake, is a truth more brilliant than the sun. The proofs of this truth are as numerous as the flowers, fruits and leaves that emerge in the spring. So the traveller said, "praise be to God for the blessing of faith."

In expression of these truths and the testimony given to them, we said in the Sixth Step of the First Station:

"There is no god but God, to the necessity of Whose Existence in Unity points the consensus of all the species of trees and plants that are engaged in glorifying God and speak with the eloquent and well-ordered words of their leaves, their loquacious and comely flowers, their well-ordered and well-spoken fruits, by the testimony of the comprehensiveness of the truth of bestowing, bounty and generosity, done in purposive mercy, and the truth of differentiation, adornment and decoration, done with will and wisdom. Definite, too, is the indication given by the truth of the opening of all of their symmetrical, adorned, distinct, variegated and infinite forms, from seeds and grains that resemble and approximate each other, that are finite and limited.''

★   ★   ★

AS THIS TRAVELLER through the cosmos proceeded on his meditative journey, with increased eagerness and a bouquet of gnosis and faith, itself like a spring, gathered from the garden of the spring, there opened before his truth-perceiving intellect, his cognitive reason, the gate to the animal and bird realm. With hundreds of thousands of different voices and various tongues, he was invited to enter. Entering, he saw that all the animals and birds, in their different species, groups and nations, were proclaiming, silently and aloud, "there is no god but He," and had thus turned the face of the earth into a vast place of invocation, an expansive assembly for the proclamation of God's glory. He saw each of them to be like an ode dedicated to God, a word proclaiming His Glory, a letter indicating His Compassion, each of them describing the Maker and offering Him thanks and encomium. It was as if the senses, powers, members and instruments of those animals and birds were orderly and balanced words, or perfect and disciplined expressions. He observed three great and comprehensive truths indicating, in decisive form, their offering of thanks to the Creator and Provider and their testimony to His Unity.

The first: their wise creation out of nothing in a fashion that in no way can be attributed to chance, to a blind force or inanimate nature; their ingenious summoning into being; their being produced in purposive and knowledgeable manner; their animation in a way that provides a twentyfold proof of knowledge, wisdom and will— all of this is a truth that bears witness to the necessary Existence of the Eternally Living and Self-Subsistent, His seven attributes and Unity, a witness repeated to the number of all animate beings.

The second: there appears from the distinction made among those infinite beings with respect to form, quantity, and shape, from their adornment and decoration, a truth so magnificent and powerful that none other than the One Powerful over all things, the One Knowledgeable of all things, could be responsible for it, and the thousands of wonders and instances of providential wisdom that it contains.

The third: the emergence of those countless creatures, in their hundreds of thousands of different shapes and forms, each of which is a miracle of wisdom, their emergence from eggs and drops of water called sperm that are identical with each other or closely resemble each other, and are limited and finite in number, all this in the most orderly, symmetrical and unfailing fashion, is so brilliant a truth as to be illumined with proofs and evidences as numerous as the animals themselves.

By the consensus of these truths, all the species of animals are engaged together in testifying that there is no god but He. It is as if the whole earth, like a great man, were saying there is no god but He, in a manner befitting its vastness, and conveying its testimony to the people of the heavens. In expression of these truths, we said in the Seventh Step of the First Station:

"There is no god but God, to whose Necessary Existence in Unity points the consensus of all animals and birds, that praise God and bear witness to Him with the words of their senses, their faculties and powers, words well-balanced, ordered and eloquent; with the words of their limbs and members, words perfect and persuasive; by the testimony of the magnificence of the comprehensiveness of the truth of bringing into being, making and creating, according to will, the truth of distinction and decoration according to purpose, and the truth of ordering and adorning according to wisdom. Definite too is the indication given by the truth of the opening of all of their orderly, distinct, variegated and infinite forms, out of identical or similar eggs and drops of sperm, that are finite and limited."

★ ★ ★

THAT MEDITATIVE VOYAGER, in order to advance farther in the infinite degrees and countless luminous stages of divine gnosis, then wished to enter the world of men, the realm of humanity.

Humanity, headed by the prophets, invited him, and he accepted the invitation. Looking first at the stopping-place of past time,˙ he saw that all of the prophets, upon whom be peace, the most luminous and perfect of human kind, were reciting in chorus, "no god but He," and making remembrance of God. With the power of their brilliant, well-attested and innumerable miracles, they were proclaiming God's unity, and in order to advance man from the animal state to angelic degree, they were instructing men and summoning them to belief in God. Kneeling down in that school of light, he too paid heed to the lesson.

He saw that in the hand of each of those teachers — the most exalted and renowned of all celebrated human beings — there were numerous miracles, bestowed on them by the Creator of All Being as a sign confirming their mission. Further, a large group of men, a whole community, had confirmed their claims and come to belief at their hands; a truth assented to and confirmed by these hundreds of thousands of serious and veracious individuals, unanimously and in full agreement, was bound to be firm and definitive. He understood, too, that the people of misguidance, in denying a truth attested and affirmed by so many veracious witnesses, were committing a most grievous error, indeed crime, and were therefore deserving of a most grievous punishment. He recognized, by contrast, those who assented to the truth and believed in it, as being the most true and righteous, and a further degree of the sanctity of belief became apparent to him.

Yes, the infinite miracles bestowed by God on the Prophets — upon whom be peace— each one being like a confirmation of their mission; the heavenly blows dealt to their opponents, each being like a proof of their truthfulness; their individual perfections, each one being like an indication of their righteousness; their veracious teachings; the strength of their faith, a witness to their honesty; their supreme seriousness and readiness to self-sacrifice; the sacred books and pages held by their hands; their countless pupils who through following their paths attain truth, perfection and light, thus proving again the truthfulness of the teachings; the unanimous agreement of the prophets — those most earnest warners — and their followers in all positive matters; their concord, mutual support and affinity — all of this constitutes so powerful a proof that no power on earth can confront it, and no doubt or hesitation can survive it.

Our traveller understood further that inclusion of belief in all the prophets — upon whom be peace — among the articles of faith, represents another great source of strength. Thus he derived great benefit of faith from their lessons, in expression of which we said in the Eighth Degree of the First Station:

"There is no god but God, to the necessity of Whose Existence in Unity points the unanimity of all the Prophets, through the power of their luminous miracles, that both affirm and are affirmed."

★ ★ ★

THAT QUESTING TRAVELLER, having derived a lofty taste of truth from the power of belief, found himself invited, while coming from the assembly of the prophets — upon whom be peace — to the classroom of those profound, original and realized ones who affirm the claims of the prophets — upon whom be peace — with the most decisive and powerful proofs and who are known as the chosen and purified ones or as the most veracious.

Entering their classroom, he saw thousands of geniuses and hundreds of thousands of exact and exalted scholars proving all the affirmative matters connected with faith, headed by the necessity of God's existence and His unity, with such profound demonstrations as to leave not the least room for doubt. Indeed, the fact that they are agreed in the principles and pillars of belief, despite their differences in capacity and outlook, and that each of them relies on a firm and certitudinous proof, is in itself such evidence that it can be doubted only if it is possible for a similar number of intelligent and perspicuous men to arrive at a single result. Otherwise the only path for the denier is to display his ignorance — his utter ignorance — and his obstinacy with respect to negative matters that admit neither of denial nor affirmation. He will in effect be closing his eyes, but the one who closes his eyes is able to turn day into night only for himself.

The traveller learned that the lights emitted in this vast and magnificent classroom by these respected and profound scholars had been illumining half of the globe for more than a thousand years. He found in it moral and spiritual force that the combined strength of all the people of denial would be unable to shake or destroy. In brief allusion to the lesson learned by the traveller in this classroom we said in the Ninth Degree of the First Station:

"There is no god but God, to Whose Necessary Existence in Unity points the agreement of all of the chosen and purified ones, with the power of their resplendent, certain and unanimous proofs."

★ ★ ★

OUR CONTEMPLATIVE TRAVELLER came forth from the classroom, ardently desiring to see the lights that are to be observed in the continuous strengthening and development of faith, and in advancing from the degree of the knowledge of certainty to that of the vision of certainty. He then found himself summoned by thousands or millions of spiritual guides who were striving toward the truth and attaining the vision of certainty in the shade of the highway and ascension of Muhammad, upon whom be peace. This they were doing in a meeting-place, a hospice, a place of remembrance and preceptorship, that was abundantly luminous and vast as a plain, being formed from the merging of countless small hospices and convents. Upon entering, he found that those spiritual guides — people of unveiling and wondrous deeds — were unanimously proclaiming, "no god but God," on the basis of their witnessing of the unseen and the wondrous deeds they had been enabled to perform; they were proclaiming the necessary existence and unity of God. The traveller observed how manifest and clear must be a truth to which unanimously subscribe these sacred geniuses and luminous gnostics, who behold the numerous luminous colors that God's pre-eternal sun manifests, just as the sun in the heavens manifests its seven colors, and who follow different true paths and various veracious patterns. This unanimity of the saints, joined to that of the prophets, upon whom be peace, and that of the chosen and pure ones, forms a supreme consensus, more brilliant than the daylight that demonstrates the existence of the sun.

In brief allusion to the benefit derived by our traveller from the Sufi hospice, we said, in the Tenth Degree of the First Station:

"There is no god but God, to whose necessary existence in unity points the unanimity of the saints in their manifest, well-affirmed and attested visionary experience and wondrous deeds."

★ ★ ★

NOW OUR TRAVELLER through the world, aware that the most important and greatest of all human perfections, indeed the very source and origin of all such perfections, is the love of God that arises from belief in God and the knowledge of God, wished with all of his powers, outer and inner, to advance still farther in the strengthening of his faith and the development of his knowledge. He therefore raised his head and gazing at the heavens said to himself:

"The most precious thing in creation is life; all things are made subordinate to life. The most precious of all living beings is the animate, and the most precious of the animate is the conscious. Each century and each year, the globe is engaged in emptying and refilling itself, in order to augment this most precious substance. It follows, then, without doubt, that the magnificent and ornate heavens must have appropriate people and inhabitants, possessing life, spirit and consciousness, for events relating to seeing and speaking with the angels — such as the appearance of Gabriel, upon whom be peace, in the presence of the Prophet, upon whom be peace, and in the view of the companions — have been transmitted and related from the most ancient times. Would, then, that I could converse with the people of the heavens, and learn their thoughts on this matter. For their words concerning the Creator of the cosmos are the most important." As he was thus thinking to himself, he suddenly heard a heavenly voice: "If you wish to meet us and hearken to our lesson, then know that before all others we have believed in the articles of faith brought by all of the prophets, headed by the Prophet Muhammad, upon whom be peace and blessings, who brought the Qur'an of Glorious Exposition.

"Then too all of the pure spirits from among us that have appeared before men have, unanimously and without exception, born witness to the necessary existence, the unity and the sacred attributes of the Creator of this cosmos, and proclaimed this with one accord. The affinity and mutual correspondence of these countless proclamations is a guide for you as bright as the sun." Thus the traveller's light of faith shone, and rose from the earth to the heavens.

In brief allusion to the lesson learned by the traveller from the angels, we said in the Eleventh Degree of the First Station:

"There is no god but God, to Whose Necessary Existence in Unity points the unanimity of the angels that appear to human gaze, and who speak to the elect among men, with their mutually corresponding and confirmed testimony."

★ ★ ★

THEN, THAT ARDENT and inquisitive traveller, having learned from the tongues of the various classes of creation in the manifest realm, desired to study and journey through the world of the unseen and the intermediate realm, and thus to attain truth. There opened before him the gate of upright and luminous intellects, of sound and

illumined hearts, that are like the seed of man —
the fruit of creation — and despite their slight
girth can expand virtually to embrace the whole
of the cosmos.

He looked and saw a series of human isthmuses
linking the realm of the unseen with that of the
manifest, and the contracts between those two
realms and the interchanges between them insofar as they affected man, taking place at those
points. Addressing his intellect and his heart he
said:

"Come, the path leading to truth from these
counterparts of yours is shorter. We should
benefit by studying the qualities, natures and
colors that we find here, not by listening to
lessons as was previously the case."

Beginning his study, he saw that the faith and
firm conviction concerning the divine unity that
all luminous intellects possessed, despite their
varying capacities and differing, even opposing,
methods and outlooks, was the same, and that
their steadfast and confident certainty and
assurance was one. They had, therefore, to be
relying on a single, unchanging truth; their roots
were sunk in a profound truth and could not
be plucked out. Their unanimity concerning faith,
the necessary existence and unity of God, was
an unbreakable and luminous chain, a brightly
lit window opening on the world of the truth.

He saw also that the unanimous, assured and
sublime unveilings and witnessings of the pillars
of faith enjoyed by all those sound and luminous
intellects, whose methods were various and out-

looks divergent, corresponded to and agreed with each other on the matter of the divine unity. All those luminous hearts, turned and joined to the truth and manifesting it, each a small throne of divine gnosis, a mirror of God's Eternal Besoughtedness, were like so many windows opened on the Sun of the Truth. Taken together, they were like a supreme mirror, like an ocean reflecting the sun. Their agreement and unanimity concerning the necessary existence and unity of God was an unfailing and reliable most perfect guide, most elevated preceptor. For it is in no way possible or conceivable that a supposition other than the truth, an untrue thought, a false attribute, should so consistently and decisively be able to deceive simultaneously so many sharp eyes, or to induce illusion in them. Not even the foolish sophists, who deny the cosmos, would agree with the corrupt and dissipated intellect that held such a thing possible. All of this our traveler understood, and he said, together with his own intellect and heart, "I have believed in God."

In brief allusion to the benefit derived from upright intellects and luminous hearts by our traveller, for knowledge of faith, we said in the Twelfth and Thirteenth Degrees of the First Station:

"There is no god but God, to Whose Necessary Existence in Unity points the consensus of all upright intellects, illumined with congruent beliefs and corresponding convictions and certainties, despite differences in capacity and outlook. There also points to His Necessary Existence in

Unity the agreement of all sound, luminous hearts, with their mutually corresponding unveilings and their congruent witnessings, despite diferences in method and manner.''

★ ★ ★

THEN THAT TRAVELLER looking closely at the world of the unseen, and voyaging in it with his intellect and his heart, knocked inquisitively on the door of that world, thinking to himself, ''what does this world have to say?'' The following occured to him: the being who wishes to make himself known in the corporeal realm of manifestation with such numerous, beautiful and ingenious products of his making; who wishes to make himself loved with so many sweet and well-adorned bounties; who wishes to reveal his secret perfections by means of so many miraculous and skilful works; who wishes all this in a manner clearer than all speech and utterance — such a being, he reasoned, must necessarily be behind the veil of the unseen. Also that being must of necessity make himself known through speech and utterance just as he does through deed and state. The traveller therefore turned to the world of the unseen and saying, ''we must come to know this being from his manifestations,'' entered it with his heart and saw the following with the eye of his intellect:

The truth of revelations prevails at all instants

over all parts of the world of the unseen, with a most powerful manifestation. There comes forth, with the truths of the revelation and inspiration proceeding from God, the Knower of the Unseen, a testimony to His existence and unity far stronger than the testimony of the cosmos and created beings. He does not abandon Himself, His existence and unity, to the testimony of His creation. Rathers He speaks with a pre-eternal speech consonant with His own being. The words of all men present in all different places, inspired with His knowledge and power, are infinite; in the same way that it is He who supplies speech with meaning, so too does the very act of speech indicate one of His attributes.

The traveller recognized that the truth of revelation has become established and been made plain to the point of being self-evident by the transmission of one hundred thousand prophets, upon whom be peace, by the agreement among their proclamations concerning the manifestation of divine revelation; by the evidences and proofs contained in the sacred books and heavenly pages that are the guides and exemplars of the overwhelming majority of humanity, confirmed and assented to by them, and that are the visible fruits of revelation. He understood further that the truth of revelation proclaims five sacred truths.

THE FIRST: to speak in accordance with men's intellects and understandings is a form of divine descent. It is a result of God's dominicality that He endows all of his conscious creatures with speech, understanding their speech, and that

He then participates in their speech with His own speech and utterance.

THE SECOND: the One who, in order to make Himself known, fills the cosmos with His miraculous creations and endows them with tongues speaking of His perfections, will necessarily make himself known with His own words also.

THE THIRD: it is part of His glory as Creator to respond in words to the discourse and offerings of thanks that are made by the most select, the most delicate and the most ardent among His creation — true men.

THE FOURTH: the attribute of speech, an essential concomitant and luminous manifestation of both knowledge and life, will necessarily be found in a comprehensive and eternal form in the being Whose knowledge is comprehensive and Whose life is eternal.

THE FIFTH: it is a consequence of divinity that the being Who endows men with impotence and desire, poverty and need, anxiety for the future, love and worship, should communicate His own existence, by way of speech, to His most loved and lovable, His most needy creation, to those who are most desirous of finding their Lord and Master.

The evidences for the existence in unity of the Necessary Existent offered in unanimity by universal and heavenly revelations, that contain the truths of divine descent, dominical self-proclamation, compassionate response, glorious discourse, and eternal self-communication, constitute a proof more powerful than the testimony for the existence of the sun brought by the rays of daylight.

Our traveller then looked in the direction of inspiration and saw that veracious inspiration indeed resembles revelation in some respects and is a mode of divine speech. There are, however, two differences.

The first: revelation, which is much higher than inspiration, generally comes by the medium of the angels, whereas inspiration generally comes directly.

So too a king has two modes of speech and command. The first consists of his sending to a governor a lieutenant equipped with all the pomp of monarchy and the splendor of sovereignty. Sometimes, in order to demonstrate the splendor of his sovereignty and the importance of his command, he may meet with the intermediary before his departure, and then the decree will be issued.

The second consists of his speaking privately in his own person, not with the title of monarch or in the name of kingship, concerning some private matter, some petty affair, using for this purpose a trusted servant, some ordinary subject, or his private telephone.

In the same way the Pre-Eternal Monarch may either, in the name of the Lord of All the Worlds, and with the title of Creator of the Cosmos, speak with revelation or the comprehensive inspiration that performs the function of revelation, or He may speak in a different and private fashion, as the Lord and Creator of all animate beings, from behind the veil, in a way suited to the recipient.

The second difference: revelation is without shadow, pure and reserved for the elect. Inspiration, by contrast, has a shadow, colors intermingle with it, and it is general. There are numerous different kinds of inspiration, such as the inspiration of angels, the inspiration of men, and the inspiration of animals; inspiration thus forms a field for the multiplication of God's words, that are as numerous as the drops in the ocean. Our traveller understood that this matter is, indeed, a kind of commentary on the verse,

> "were the sea to become ink for the words of my Lord, verily the sea would be exhausted before the words of my Lord.[13]"

Then he looked at the nature, the wisdom and the testimony of inspiration and saw that its nature, wisdom and result were composed of four lights.

The first: it is the result of God's Lovingness and Compassionateness that He makes himself loved through word, presence and discourse, in the same way that He makes himself loved to His creatures through His deeds.

The second: it is a requirement of His mercifulness that just as He answers His servant's prayers in deed, He should also answer them in word, from behind veils.

13. Qur'an 18:109

The third: it is a concomitant of dominicality that just as He responds in deed to the cries for help, supplications and pleadings of those of His creatures who are afflicted with grievous misfortunes and hardships, so too He should hasten to their help with words of inspiration, which are like a form of speech.

The fourth: God makes His existence, presence and protection perceptible in deed to His most weak and indigent, His most poor and needy, animate and conscious creation, that stands in great need of finding its Master, Protector, Guardian and Disposer. It is a necessary and essential consequence of His divine solicitousness and His dominical compassion that He should also communicate His presence and existence by speech, from behind the veil of veracious inspiration — a mode of divine discourse — to individuals, in a manner peculiar to them and their capacities, through the telephone of their hearts.

He then looked to the testimony of inspiration and saw that if the sun, for example, had consciousness and life, and if the seven colors of sunlight were seven attributes, the rays and flashes of the light would speak in a single fashion. The light would be found in transparent objects, both similar and dissimilar, and it would, as it were, be speaking to every mirror and resplendent object, to every piece of glass and every drop, to every transparent atom, in accordance with the capacity of each. The light would thus respond to the needs of each, and they in turn would bear witness to the existence of the sun, without one task interfering with the other, or one discourse conflicting with the other. In the same way the speech of the Glorious Monarch of Pre-and Post-Eternity, the Beauteous and Exalted Creator of All Beings, Who may be designated as the Eternal Sun, manifests itself to all things, in general and comprehensive fashion, in a manner appropriate to the capacity of all things, as do also His knowledge and power. No request interferes with another, no task prevents the fulfillment of another, and no address becomes confused with another. All of this our traveller understood as self-evident. He knew that all of those manifestations, discourses, and inspirations, separately and together, evidenced and bore witness unanimously to the presence and necessary existence and unity of that Pre-eternal Sun with a knowledge of certainty that approached a vision of certainty.

In brief allusion to the lesson of gnosis gained by our inquisitive traveller from the world of the unseen, we said in the Fourteenth and Fifteenth Degrees of the First Station:

"There is no god but God, to Whose Necessary Existence in Unity points the consensus of all true revelations, containing divine descent, glorious discourse, dominical self-revelation, compassionate response to the invocations of men, and eternal intimations of His existence to His creatures. There points also to His Necessary Existence in Unity the agreement of all veracious inspirations, containing expressions of God's love, compassionate responses to the prayers of God's creatures, dominical responses to the appeals of His servants for aid, and glorious communications of His existence to His creatures.''

★　★　★

THEN THAT TRAVELLER through the world addressed his own intellect saying: "Since I am seeking my Master and Creator by means of the creatures of the cosmos, I ought before all else to visit the most celebrated of all these creatures, the greatest and most accomplished commander among them, according to the testimony even of his enemies, the most renowned judge, the most exalted in speech and the most brilliant an intellect, who has illuminated fourteen centuries with his excellence and with his Qur'an, Muhammad the Arabian Prophet, may God's peace and blessings be upon him." In order thus to visit him and seek from him the answer to his quest, he entered the blessed age of the Prophet in his mind, and saw that age to be one of true felicity, thanks to that being. For through the light he had brought, he had turned the most primitive and illiterate of peoples into the masters and teachers of the world.

He said too to his own intellect, "Before asking him concerning our Creator, we should first learn the value of this extraordinary being, the veracity of his words and the truthfulness of his warnings." Thus he began investigating, and of the numerous conclusive proofs that he found we will briefly indicate here only nine of the most general ones.

THE FIRST: All excellent qualities and characteristics were to be found in that extraordinary being, according to the testimony even of his enemies. Hundreds of miracles were made manifest at his hands, according to explicit Qur'anic verses or traditions enjoying the status of *tawatur*[14]. Examples of these miracles are his splitting of the moon —"And the moon split[15]"— with a single indication of his finger; his casting of a handful of dust into the eyes of his enemies, causing them to flee—"It was not thy act when thou threwest, but God's[16]"— and his giving his thirsting army to drink from the water that flowed forth from his five fingers like the spring of *Kauthar*[17]. Since some of those miracles, numbering more than three hundred, have been set forth with decisive proofs in the remarkable and wondrous work known as *The Miracles of Muhammad (Nineteenth Letter),* we leave discussion of the miracles to that book, and permit the traveller to continue speaking:

"A being who in addition to his noble characteristics and perfections has all these luminous miracles to demonstrate, must certainly be the most truthful in speech of all men. It is inconceivable that he would stoop to trickery, lies and error, the deeds of the vile."

---

14. *Tawatur* is the kind of report that is transmitted by numerous authorities and about which there is no room for doubt (Trans).

15. Qur'an 54:1

16. Qur'an 8:17

17. A river in Paradise.

THE SECOND: He holds in his hand a decree from the Lord of creation, a decree accepted and affirmed in each century by more than three hundred million people. This decree, the Qur'an of Mighty Stature, is wondrous in seven different ways. The fact that the Qur'an has forty different aspects of miraculousness and that it is the word of the Creator of all beings has been set forth in detail with strong proofs in the *Twenty-Fifth Word — the Miracles of the Qur'an,* a celebrated treatise that is like the sun of *the Risale-i Nur.* We therefore leave such matters to that work and listen to the traveller as he says, "There can never be any possibility of lying on the part of the being who is the conveyor and proclaimer of this decree, for that would be a violation of the decree and treachery toward the One Who issued it."

THE THIRD: Such a Sacred Law, an Islam, a code of worship, a cause, a summons, and a faith did that being bring forth that the like of them does not exist, nor could it exist. Nor does a more perfect form of them exist, nor could it exist. For the Law appearing with that unlettered being has no rival in its administration of one fifth of humanity for fourteen centuries, in a just and precise manner through its numerous injunctions. Moreover the Islam that emerged from the deeds, sayings, and inward states of that unlettered being has no peer, nor can it have, for in each century it has been for three hundred million men a guide and a refuge, the teacher and educator of their intellects and the illuminator and purifier of their hearts, the cause for the refinement and training of their souls, and the source of progress and advancement of their spirits.

The Prophet is similarly unparalleled in the way in which he was the foremost in practising all the forms of worship found in his religion, and the first in piety and the fear of God; in his observing the duties of worship fully and with attention to their profoundest dimensions, even while engaged in constant struggle and activity; in his practice of worship without imitation of anyone, combining in perfect fashion the beginning and the end of spiritual progress.

With the *Jaushan al-Kabir,* from among his thousands of supplicatory prayers and petitions, he describes his Lord with such a degree of gnosis that all the gnostics and saints who have come after him have been unable, with their joint efforts, to attain a similar degree of gnosis and accurate description. This shows that in prayer too he is without peer. Whoever looks at the section at the beginning of the *Treatise on Supplicatory Prayer* which sets forth some part of the meaning of one of the ninety-nine sections of the *Jaushan al-Kabir* will say that there is no form of supplicatory prayer like the *Jaushan.*

In his conveying of the message and his summoning men to the truth, he displayed such steadfastness, firmness and courage that although great states and religions, and even his own people, tribe and uncle opposed him in the most hostile fashion, he exhibited not the slightest trace of hesitation, anxiety or fear. The fact that he successfully challenged the whole world and made Islam the master of the world likewise proves that there is not and cannot be anyone like him in his conveying of the message and summons.

In his faith, he had so extraordinary a strength, so marvellous a certainty, so miraculous a breadth, and so exalted a conviction, illumining the whole world, that none of the ideas and beliefs then dominating the world, and none of the philosophies of the sages and teachings of the spiritual chiefs, was able, despite extreme hostility and denial, to induce in his certainty, conviction, trust and assurance, the slightest doubt, hesitation, weakness or anxiety. Moreover, the saintly of all ages, headed by the Companions, the foremost in the degrees of belief, have all drawn on his fountain of belief and regarded him as representing the highest degree of faith. This proves that his faith too is matchless. Our traveller therefore concluded, and affirmed with his intellect, that lying and duplicity have no place in the one who has brought such a unique sacred law, such an unparalleled Islam, such a wondrous devotion to worship, such an extraordinary excellence in supplicatory prayer, such a universally acclaimed summons to the truth and such a miraculous faith.

THE FOURTH: In the same way that the consensus of the prophets is a strong proof for the existence and oneness of God, so too it is a firm testimony to the truthfulness and messengerhood of this being. For all the sacred attributes, miracles and functions that indicate the truthfulness and messengerhood of the prophets, upon whom be peace, existed in fullest measure in that being, according to the testimony of history. The prophets have verbally predicted the coming of that being and given good tidings thereof in the Torah, the Gospels, the Psalms and the pages; more than twenty of the most conclusive examples of these glad tidings, drawn from the scriptures, have been set forth and proven in the *Nineteenth Letter.*

Similarly, through all the deeds and miracles associated with their prophethood they have affirmed and — as it were — put their signature to the mission of that being who is the foremost and most perfect in the tasks and functions of prophethood. Just as through verbal consensus they indicate the Divine oneness, through the unanimity of their deeds they bear witness to the truthfulness of that being. This too was understood by our traveller.

THE FIFTH: Similarly, the thousands of saints who have attained truth, reality, perfection, wondrous deeds, unveiling and witnessing through the instruction of this being and following him, bear unanimous witness not only to the Divine oneness but also to the truthfulness and messengerhood of this being. Again, the fact that they witness, through the light of sainthood, some of the truths he proclaimed concerning the world of the Unseen, and that they believe in and affirm all of those truths, either by the light of faith, by the knowledge of certainty, by the essence of certainty, or by the truth of certainty — this too demonstrates like the sun the degree of truthfulness and rectitude of that great being.

THE SIXTH: The millions of purified, sincere and punctilious scholars and faithful sages, who have reached the highest station of learning through the teaching and instruction contained in the sacred truths brought by that being, despite his unlettered nature, the exalted sciences he invented and the divine knowledge he discovered — they not only prove and affirm, unanimously and with the strongest proofs, the Divine unity which is the foundation of his mission, but also bear unanimous witness to the truthfulness of this Supreme Teacher and Great Guide, and to the veracity of his words. This is a proof as clear as daylight. *The Risale-i Nur,* too, with its one hundred parts, is but a single proof of his truthfulness.

THE SEVENTH: The Family and Companions of the Prophet — who with their insight, knowledge and spiritual accomplishment are the most renowned, the most respected, the most celebrated, the most pious and the most keensighted of men after the prophets — examined and scrutinized, with the utmost attention, seriousness and exactitude, all the states, thoughts and conditions of this being, whether hidden or open. They came to the unanimous conclusion that he was the most truthful, exalted and honest being in the world, and this, their unshakeable affirmation and firm belief, is a proof like the daylight attesting the reality of the sun.

THE EIGHTH: The cosmos indicates the Maker, Inscriber, and Designer, Who makes of it a palace, a book, an exhibition, a spectacle. In the same way an exalted demonstrator, a truthful unveiler, a learned master and a truthful teacher, who knows and makes known the Divine purposes inherent in creation, who demonstrates the dominical wisdom residing in the changes of the cosmos, who teaches the result of its purposeful motions, and who expounds the meanings of that supreme book — since his existence is demanded and necessary, and his functions indicate his truthfulness, he is the most exalted and truthful officer of the Creator of the cosmos.

THE NINTH: There is behind the veil One Who wishes to demonstrate with these ingenious and wise artefacts the perfection of His talent and art; to make Himself known and loved by means of these countless adorned and decorated creations; to evoke praise and thanks through the unnumbered pleasurable and valuable bounties that He bestows; to cause men to worship Him with gratitude and appreciation for His dominicality, through His solicitous and protective sustenance of life, and His provision of nurture and bounty in such manner as to satisfy the most delicate of tastes and appetites; to manifest His divinity through the change of seasons, the alternation of night and day, and through all His magnificent and majestic deeds, all His awe-inspiring and wise acts and creativity, and thereby to cause men to believe in His divinity, in submission, humility and obedience; and to demonstrate His justice and truthfulness by at all times protecting virtue and the virtuous and destroying evil and the evil, by annihilating with blows from heaven the oppressor and the liar. There will of a certainty be at the side of this Unseen Being His most beloved creation and most devoted bondsman, who, serving the

purposes that have just been mentioned, discovers
and unravels the talisman and riddle of being,
who acts always in the name of that Being, who
seeks aid and success from Him, and who receives
them from Him — Muhammad of Quraish, peace
and blessings be upon him!

The traveller further said, addressing his own
intellect: "Since these nine truths bear witness to
the truthfulness of this being, he must be the
source of glory of mankind and the source of
honor for the world. If we therefore call him the
Pride of the World and the Glory of the Sons of
Adam, it will be fitting. The fact that the awesome
sovereignty of that decree of the Compassionate
One, the Qur'an of Miraculous Exposition that he
holds in his hand, has conquered half the world,
together with his individual perfections and exalted
virtues, shows that he is the most important
personage in the world. The most important word
concerning our Creator is that which he utters."

Now see: the foundation of the summons of this
extraordinary being and the aim of all his life,
based on the strength furnished by his hundreds
of evident and manifest miracles, and the thousands of exalted, fundamental truths contained in
his religion, was to prove and bear witness to the
existence of the Necessary Existent, His unity, attributes and names, to affirm, proclaim and announce Him. He is therefore like a sun in the
cosmos, the most brilliant proof of our Creator,
this being whom we call the Beloved of God.
There are three forms of great and infallible consensus each of which affirms, confirms and puts

its signature to the witness he bears.

THE FIRST: the unanimous affirmation made by that luminous assembly known and celebrated throughout the world as the Family of Muhammad — peace and blessings be upon him — including thousands of poles and supreme saints of penetrating gaze and ability to perceive the Unseen, such as Imam Ali — may God be pleased with him — who said, "Were the veil to be lifted, my certainty would not increase," and Abdul Qadir Gilani Ghauth al-A'zam — may his secret be sanctified — who saw the Supreme Throne and the awesome form of Gabriel while yet on the earth.

THE SECOND: the confirmation made with a strong faith that permitted men to sacrifice their lives and their property, their fathers and tribes, by the renowned assembly known as the Companions, who found themselves among a primitive people and in an unlettered environment, devoid of all social life and political thought, without any scripture and lost in the darkness of a period between prophets; and who in a very brief time came to be the masters, guides, and just rulers of the most civilized and politically and socially advanced peoples and states, and to rule the world from east to west in universally approved fashion.

THE THIRD: the confirmation provided with unanimous and certain knowledge by that lofty group of punctilious and profound scholars of whom in each age thousands spring forth, who advance in wondrous fashion in every art and work in different fields.

The testimony brought by this being to the Divine oneness is not particular and individual, but general and universal and unshakeable. If all the demons that exist were to unite, they could not challenge it. Such was the conclusion reached by the traveller.

In reference to the lesson learned in the School of Light by that traveller from the world, that wayfarer in life, when he visited in his mind the blessed age of the Prophet, we said at the end of the Sixteenth Degree of the First Station:

"There is no god but God, the Necessary Existent, the One, the Unique, the Necessity of Whose Existence in Unity is indicated by the Pride of the World and the Glory of the Sons of Adam, through the majesty of the sovereignty of his Qur'an, the splendor of the expanse of his religion, the multiplicity of his perfections, and the exaltedness of his characteristics, as confirmed even by the testimony of his enemies. He bears witness and brings proof through the strength of his hundreds of manifest and evident miracles, that both testify to truth and are themselves the object of true testimony; and through the strength of the thousands of luminous and conclusive truths contained in his religion, according to the consensus of all the possessors of light, the agreement of his illumined Companions, and the unanimity of the scholars of his community, the possessors of proof and luminous insight."

★ ★ ★

THE TIRELESS and insatiable traveller, who knew
the aim of life in this world and the essence of life
to be faith, addressed his own heart and said: "Let
us examine the book known as the Qur'an of
Miraculous Exposition, which is said to be the
word and utterance of the Being Whom we are
seeking, the most famous, the most brilliant and
wisest book in the world, that issues a challenge
in every age to whoever refuses to submit to it.
Let us see what it says. But first, we must establish
that this book is from our Creator."

Since the traveller lived in the present age, he
looked first at the *Risale-i Nur,* flashes from the
miraculousness of the Qur'an; he saw its one
hundred and thirty parts to consist of luminous
points drawn from that Book of Discernment, or
well-founded explanations of its contents. Even
though the *Risale-i Nur* is valiantly struggling to
diffuse the truths of the Qur'an in all directions,
in this obstinate and atheistic age, no one can de-
feat it, which proves that its master, its source, its
authority and its sun, is the Qur'an, heavenly not
human speech. Among the hundreds of proofs in
the different parts of the *Risale-i Nur*, the single
proof contained in the Twenty-Fifth Word and
the end of the *Nineteenth Letter,* establishes forty
aspects of the Qur'an's miraculousness in such a
way that whoever sees it, far from uttering any
criticism or objection, admires its arguments, and
utters appreciative praise. The traveller left it to the
Risale-i Nur to prove that the Qur'an is miraculous
and the true word of God, turning only to a brief
indication of a few points indicating its greatness.

FIRST POINT: just as the Qur'an, with all its miracles and truths indicating its veracity is a miracle of Muhammad, upon whom be peace and blessings, so too, Muhammad, upon whom be peace and blessings, with all his miracles, proofs of prophethood and perfections of knowledge, is a miracle of the Qur'an, and a decisive proof of the Qur'an's being the word of God.

SECOND POINT: the Qur'an, in this world, brought about, in so luminous, felicitous and truthful a fashion, a revolution in the social life of man, as well as in the souls, hearts, spirits, and intellects of men, in their individual, social and political lives, and having caused this revolution, perpetuated it in such a fashion, that for fourteen centuries at every moment its six thousand, six hundred and sixty-six verses have been read by the tongues of more than a hundred million men, training them, refining their souls and purifying their hearts. To spirits, it has been a means of development and advancement; to intellects, an orientation and a light; to life, it has been life itself and felicity. Such a book is of a certainty unparalleled; it is a wonder, a marvel, and a miracle.

THIRD POINT: The Qur'an, from that age down to the present, has demonstrated such eloquence that it caused the value attached to the odes known as "Seven Hanging Poems" that were written in gold on the walls of the Ka'ba to descend to such a point that the daughter of Labid, when taking down her father's poem from the Ka'ba, said, "compared with the verses of the Qur'an, this no longer has any value."

A beduin poet heard a certain verse being recited and immediately prostrated. They asked him:

"have you become a Muslim?" "No," he said, "I was prostrating in front of the eloquence of this verse[18]"

Thousands of scholars and litterateurs, like geniuses of the science of rhetoric such as Abdul-qahir Jurjani, Sakkaki and Zamakhshari, have unanimously decided that the eloquence of the Qur'an is beyond human capacity and is unattainable.

The Qur'an has also from that time forward invited to the field of combat all arrogant and egoistic litterateurs and rhetoricians, and said to them in a manner calculated to break their arrogance: "Come, produce a single sura like unto it ..or else accept perdition and humiliation in this world and the hereafter." Despite this challenge, the obstinate rhetoricians of that age abandoned the short path of producing a single sura like the Qur'an, and instead chose the long path of casting their persons and property in danger. This proves that the short path cannot be taken.

Millions of Arabic books are in circulation, some written by friends of the Qur'an in order to resemble and imitate it, others written by its enemies in order to confront and criticize it. If the most common man hears that not one of them was able to attain the level of the Qur'an, he will naturally say: "the Qur'an does not resemble these other

18. Qur'an 15:94

books, nor is it in the same class as they. It must be either below them or above them." No one — no unbeliever or fool — in the world can say that it is below them. Hence its degree of eloquence is above all of them. Once a man read the verse,

> "there gives glory to God all that is in the heavens and the earth[19]"

He said: "I cannot see any miraculous eloquence in this verse." He was told: "Go back to that age like the traveller, and listen to the verse as recited there." Imagining himself to be there before the revelation of the Qur'an, he saw that all the beings in the world, were living in an empty, infinite and unbounded space, in an unstable, transient world, in confusion, darkness, a lack of consciousness and purpose. Suddenly he heard this verse proclaimed by the tongue of the Qur'an, and the verse removed a veil from in front of the cosmos and illumined the face of the globe; this pre-eternal speech, this eternal command gave instruction to all conscious beings, drawn up in the ranks of succeeding centuries, in such fashion that the cosmos became like a vast mosque. All of creation, headed by the heavens and the earth, was engaged in vital remembrance of God and proclamation of His glory, was joyously and contentedly fulfilling its function. All of this our traveller observed. Thus tasting the degree of the eloquence of the Qur'an, and comparing the other verses to it by analogy, he understood one of the many thousands

19. Qur'an 57:1

of wise reasons for the conquest of half the globe and a fifth of humanity by the eloquent murmuring of the Qur'an, for the uninterrupted continuance of its respected and magnificent monarchy for fourteen centuries.

FOURTH POINT: The Qur'an has demonstrated such a veracious sweetness that whereas the repetition of even the sweetest thing induces disgust, it has from earliest times been accepted by everyone and even become proverbial that repeated recitation of the Qur'an, far from inducing disgust and weariness in men of sound heart and pure taste, on the contrary increases its sweetness.

The Qur'an demonstrates, moreover, such a freshness, youth and originality, that even though it has lived for fourteen centuries and passed through many hands, it retains its freshness as if it had only just been revealed. Every century sees the Qur'an enjoying a new youth, as if it were addressing that century in particular. Similarly, every branch of learning, even though it keeps the Qur'an constantly at its side in order to benefit from it, and perpetually follows the same method of reference, sees that the Qur'an maintains the originality of its style and method of exposition.

THE FIFTH POINT: the Qur'an has one wing in the past, and one wing in the future. Its roots are in the unanimous truths proclaimed by the earlier prophets, which confirm and strengthen it. So too the fruits that gain life from the Qur'an — the saints and the chosen and pure ones — all the true Sufi paths and all the veracious sciences of Islam that indicate the vitality, abundance and veracity of that blessed tree, with their vital evolution, and live in the protection of the second wing of Islam — all of these bear witness to the Qur'an being truth itself, a compendium of verities, an unparalleled miracle.

THE SIXTH POINT: the six directions of the Qur'an are all luminous; they all demonstrate truthfulness and veracity. Beneath it are the pillars of argument and proof; above it glisten the jewels of miraculousness; in front of it is its goal, the happiness of both worlds; behind it is its support, the truths of heavenly revelation; to its right is confirmation by evidences adduced by countless sound intelligences; to its left is the earnest assurance and sincere submission of sound hearts and unsullied consciences. These six, taken together, prove that the Qur'an is an extraordinarily miraculous, firm and impregnable castle, that stretches from earth up to heaven. Then too the controller of this cosmos whose constant rule of conduct it is to make manifest the beauty in creation, to protect goodness and honesty, and to destroy and eradicate falsehood and lying — He has attested to the fact that the Qur'an is truth itself, is veracious, is not man's word nor subject to error; He has awarded the Qur'an the most desirable, the highest, the most dominant station of respect and degree of veneration in the world. Then there is this, that the source of Islam and the interpreter of the Qur'an, peace and blessings be upon him, believed in it and respected it more than anyone else. Sometimes revelation would come to him while he was asleep and impervious to other words, but despite his unlettered nature, he set forth unhesitatingly and with the utmost confidence true proclamations concerning past and future, by means of the Qur'an. This he did under the scrutiny of attentive eyes, but no error was observed in him. He believed in and assented to every ordinance of the Qur'an and nothing was able to shake him; this, too, constitutes a proof of the heavenly and veracious nature of the Qur'an, of the fact that it is the blessed word of a Merciful Creator.

The pious and rapturous attachment of one fifth of humanity, or even the major part of humanity, to the Qur'an, the ardent, truth-worshipping heed they pay to its commands; the fact that, by the testimony of numerous indications, visions and unveilings, jinn, angels, and spirit-beings gather like moths wherever the Qur'an is being recited — this is an indication that the Qur'an is the most widely accepted book in the cosmos and occupies the highest place of respect.

The fact that all classes of men, from the lowest and most ignorant to the most learned and intelligent, derive full benefit from the lesson of the Qur'an and comprehend its most profound truths; and the fact that each class of scholars, concerned with the hundreds of different branches of Islamic science, and especially the scholars of the Sacred Law, of the principles of religion and the science of theology, find their needs fulfilled and their questions answered by the Qur'an — this is a proof that the Qur'an is a source of truth and a mine of veracity.

Among the litterateurs of the Arabs, the most accomplished people in rhetoric, those who have not embraced Islam have failed up to the present to produce a single sura like in eloquence to those of the Qur'an, the eloquence of the Qur'an being merely one of seven aspects of its miraculousness, this, despite their great need to meet the challenge of the Qur'an. In addition, the celebrated rhetoricians and talented scholars who have wished to gain fame by raising objections have been unable to confront even a single aspect of the miraculousness of the Qur'an and instead have remained silent. All of this is a further indication that the Qur'an is a miracle and beyond human capacity.

The worth, exaltedness and eloquence of words is to be measured by knowing from whom they came, to whom they came, and for what purpose they came, and from this point of view the Qur'an is without peer and is unattainable. For the Qur'an is an address and a speech by the Lord and Creator of all the worlds, an utterance devoid of any sign that might indicate the possibility of artifice or imitation. It is addressed to one who is delegated to represent all men, or even all creatures, the most celebrated and famous of human kind, the strength and breadth of whose faith gave rise to Islam and elevated him to the station of "the distance of two bowstrings." It expounds and clarifies the most elevated and expansive faith, one that contains all matters related to felicity in this world and the hereafter, the consequences of the creation of the cosmos and the dominical purposes

inherent therein, and all the truths of Islam. It
shows every corner of creation like a map, a watch
or a house, and expresses and gives instruction in
all this in the tongue of the Maker himself. It is
then naturally impossible to produce the like of the
Qur'an of Miraculous Exposition, or to attain its
degree of miraculousness.

Then, too, the countless excellences of the
Qur'an, its subtle points, properties, mysteries and
exalted meanings, as well as its numerous predic-
tions of matters belonging to the unseen, expounded, proven and asserted with proofs and evidences by thousands of expert scholars of high
intelligence and perspicacity, who have written
commentaries on the Qur'an in thirty, forty, or
even seventy volumes; especially the excellences and
subtleties of the Qur'an established each with
decisive arguments in one of the hundred and
thirty parts of the *Risale-i Nur,* particularly the
Treatise on the Miracles of the Qur'an (the Second
Station of the Twentieth Word) which deduces the
railway, the airplane and many of the wonders of
civilization from the text of the Qur'an, the First
Ray (The Qur'anic Indications) that demonstrates
the indications of the *Risale-i Nur* and electricity
contained in the Qur'an, the eight brief treatises
(called the Eight Mysteries) that show how well-
shaped and imbued with mystery and meaning are
the letters of the Qur'an, and the brief treatises
demonstrating five aspects of the miraculousness
of the last verse of *Surat al-Fath,* as well as the
truth and light of the Qur'an that is contained in
each part of the *Risale-i Nur* — all of the foregoing

is an indication of the uniqueness of the Qur'an, of the fact that it is a miracle and a marvel, the tongue of the unseen world come to the manifest world, the speech of One Endowed with Knowledge of the Unseen.

It is on account of the aforementioned excellences and properties of the Qur'an, indicated in six points, six directions and six stations, that its magnificent and luminous sovereignty, its splendid and sacred authority, has been continually illumining the face of the earth for thirteen hundred years and receiving the utmost respect. It is again on account of these properties that each letter of the Qur'an has gained the distinction of bestowing at least ten rewards, ten requitals and ten everlasting fruits. Indeed, each letter of certain verses and suras yields a hundred, a thousand or more fruits, and at certain blessed times the light, reward and value of each letter rises from ten to a thousand. The traveller perceived this and said to his heart:

"The Qur'an that is thus miraculous in every respect, through the consensus of its suras, the agreement of its verses, the congruence of its lights and mysteries and the correspondence of its fruits and effects, bears witness to the existence, unity, attributes and names of the Necessary Existent in such evidential fashion that the infinite witness of all the people of faith may be said to have proceeded from it."

In brief allusion to the lesson on divine unity and faith the traveller derived from the Qur'an, it was said in the Seventeenth Degree of the First Station:

"There is no god but God, the One and Unique Necessary Existent, to Whose Necessary Existence in Unity points the Qur'an of Miraculous Exposition, the book accepted and desired by all species of angel, men and jinn, whose verses are read each minute of the year, with the utmost reverence, by hundreds of millions of men, whose sacred sovereignty over the regions of earth and the universe and the face of time is permanent, whose spiritual and luminous authority has run over half the earth and a fifth of humanity, for more than fourteen centuries, with the utmost splendor. Testimony and proof is also given by the unanimity of its sacred and heavenly suras, the agreement of its luminous, divine verses, the congruence of its mysteries and lights, the correspondence of its fruits and effects and truths, by witnessing and clear vision."

★ ★ ★

OUR TRAVELLER, our voyager through life, knew now that faith is the most precious capital man can have, for it bestows on indigent man not some transient and ephemeral field or dwelling, but a palace, indeed an eternal kingdom as vast as the whole cosmos or the world itself. Faith also bestows on ephemeral man all he will need for life eternal; delivers from eternal annihilation wretched man who waits on the gallows for the arrival of fate; and opens to man an eternal treasury of everlasting felicity. The traveller then said to himself:

"Onward! In order to gain a further degree from among the infinite degrees of faith, let us refer to the total plan of the cosmos, and listen to what it says. We will then be able to perfect and illumine the lessons we have received from its components and parts."

Looking through the broad and comprehensive telescope he had taken from the Qur'an, he saw the cosmos to be so meaningful and well-ordered that it took on the shape of a personified book of the Glorious One, an incarnate Dominical Qur'an, a finely adorned city of the Compassionate One. All the suras, verses and words of that book, even its very letters, chapters, divisions, pages and lines, through their constant meaningful effacement and reaffirmation, their wise changes and alternations, gave unanimous expression to the existence and presence of One Knowledgeable of all things and Empowered over all things as the author of the book, of a Glorious Inscriber and a Perfect Scribe seeing all things in all things and knowing the relationship of all things with all things. So, too, all the species and particles of the cosmos, all its inhabitants and contents, all that enters it and leaves it, all the providential changes and the wise processes of rejuvenation that occur in it — these proclaim in unison the existence and unity of an exhalted craftsman, a peerless Maker who sets to work with limitless power and infinite wisdom. The testimony of two great and vast truths, of a piece with the greatness and vastness of the cosmos, affirms this supreme witness of the cosmos.

THE FIRST TRUTH: there are the truths of createdness and contingency established with countless proofs by the gifted scholars of the principles of religion and the science of theology, as well as the sages of Islam. They said that since change and mutation are to be observed in the world and all things, the world must be ephemeral and created; it cannot be uncreated. If it is created, then there must be a Maker who created it. And if there is no cause to be found in the essence of a thing either for its being or for its non-being, so that these two are equally possible, that thing cannot be necessary and eternal.

It has further been proven with decisive arguments that it is not possible for things to create each other, since that would involve the absurd and false notion of delegation and substantial continuity. Hence the existence of a Necessary Existent becomes necessary, whose like cannot exist, whose similitude is impossible, all other than whom is contingent and created by him.

Yes, the truth of createdness has permeated the whole of the cosmos, and many instances of it are visible to the eye; the rest can be seen only by the intellect. For in front of our eyes a whole world dies every autumn, and together with it die hundreds of thousands of different kinds of plants and small animals, each member of each species being like a small cosmos unto himself. It is, however, so orderly and disciplined a death that all things leave behind in their places seeds and eggs that in the spring shall be the means of resurrection and rebirth, miracles of mercy and wisdom, miracles of power and knowledge. They hand to the seeds and eggs their book of deeds and plan of action, entrusting them to them under the protection of the Glorious Guardian, and only then do they die.

In spring, the dead trees, roots and animals come to life again exactly as they were, thus providing hundreds of thousands of examples, specimens and proofs of the supreme resurrection. In the place of others, plants and animals resembling them exactly are brought into being and life, thus publishing the pages of the beings of the preceding spring, together with their deeds and functions, just like an advertisement. Thus they demonstrate one meaning of the verse,

"when the pages are spread out[20]"

Then also, with respect to the whole, each autumn a great world dies, and each spring a fresh world comes into being. That death and creation proceed in so orderly a manner, and so many separate deaths and creations occur within them, in such orderly and regular fashion, that it is as if the world were a traveller's lodge where animate beings reside for a time, where travelling worlds and migrant realms come, fulfill their duties, and then go on their way.

So there is apparent to all intellects, with the clarity of the sun, the necessary existence, infinite power and unending wisdom of a Glorious Being Who creates and brings into being in this world vital realms and purposive beings, with per-

20. Qur'an 81:10

fect wisdom, knowledge and equilibrium, with
balance, order and regularity, and who then
employs them for dominical purposes, divine aims
and compassionate goals, with full power and
mercy. We leave to the *Risale-i Nur* and the books
of the theologians the further discussion of matters
related to createdness.

As for contingence, it prevails over and sur-
rounds all of the cosmos. For we see that all
things, universal or particular, big or small, from
God's throne down to the ground, from the atom
to the planet, all are sent to the world with a particular essence, a specific form, a distinct identity,
particular attributes, wise qualities, and beneficial
organs. Now to bestow on that particular essence
and quiddity its peculiarities, from amongst the
infinite possibilities available; to clothe it in its
specific, distinctive and appropriate form, from
among the possibilities and probabilities that are
as numerous as the forms that may be conceived;
to distinguish that being with the identity suited
to it, from among the possibilities as numerous as
the other members of its species; to endow with
special, suitable and beneficial attributes the
created object that is formless and hesitant amidst
the possibilities and probabilities that are as
numerous as the varieties of attribute and degree;
to affix to that aimless creature, perplexed and distraught amidst the innumerable possibilities and
probabilities that result from the infinitude of conceivable paths and modalities — to affix to him
wise qualities and beneficial organs and equip him
with them ; — all of these are indications, proofs

and affirmations of the necessary existence, infinite power and unlimited wisdom of the Necessary Existent Who delineates, arranges and specifies the quiddity and identity, the form and shape, the attribute and situation of all contingent beings, whether they be universals or particulars. They indicate, too, that no object and no matter is hidden from Him, that nothing is difficult for Him, that the greatest task is as easy for Him as the smallest, that He can create a spring as easily as a tree, and a tree as easily as a seed. All this, then, pertains to the truth of contingence, and forms one wing of the great testimony born by the cosmos.

Since the testimony of the cosmos, with its two wings and two truths, is fully established and explained in various parts of the *Risale-i Nur,* and particularly the Twenty-Second and Thirty-Second Words, as well as the Twentieth and Thirty-Third Letters, we refer our readers to those writings, and cut short an extremely long story.

As for the second truth that proceeds from the total scheme of the cosmos, which is also the second wing of its great and universal testimony, it is as follows:

There is to be seen a truth of cooperation among these beings that are attempting singly to maintain their existence and fulfill their functions in the midst of constantly stirring changes and revolutions, a truth that lies far beyond their capacities.

For example, the elements hasten to aid animate beings; the clouds, to help the vegetable kingdom; the vegetable kingdom, to help the animal kingdom; the animal kingdom, to help the human kingdom. Milk gushes forth from the breast, like the spring of paradise, to succor the infant; the fact that animate beings are given their needs and sustenance in a manner that transcends their capacity, in unexpected places; the replenishing of the cells of the body with particles of food, through their submission to God and their employment at His Compassionate Hands — all of these and numerous other examples of the truth of cooperation demonstrate the universal and merciful dominicality of the Lord of the Worlds Who administers the cosmos like a palace.

Solid, inanimate and unfeeling objects, that nonetheless cooperate with each other in a sensitive and conscious fashion, must of necessity be caused to rush to each other's aid by the power, compassion and command of a Merciful, Wise and Glorious Lord.

The universal cooperation visible throughout the cosmos; the comprehensive equilibrium prevailing with the utmost regularity in all things, from the planets to the members, limbs and bodily particles of animate beings; the adornment whose pen ranges over the gilded face of the heavens, the decorated face of the earth, and the delicate faces of flowers; the order that prevails over all things, from the milky way and the solar system down to fruits such as corn and pomegranate; the assignment of duties to all things, from the sun and the moon, the elements and the clouds, down to honey bees — all of these great truths offer a testimony of proportionate greatness, and their testimony forms the second wing of the testimony offered by the cosmos.

Since the *Risale-i Nur* has established and clarified this great testimony, we will content ourselves here with this brief indication.

In brief allusion to the lesson of faith learned by our traveller from the cosmos, we said in the Eighteenth Degree of the First Station:

"There is no god but God, the Necessary Existent, the like of Whom cannot exist, other than Whom all things are contingent, the One, the Unique, to the Necessity of Whose Existence in Unity points the cosmos, the great book incarnate, the supreme Qur'an personified, the ornate and orderly palace, the splendid and well-arranged city, with all of its suras, verses, letters, chapters, parts, pages and lines, with the agreement of its fundaments, species, parts and particles its inhabitants and contents, what enters it and what leaves it; with the testimony of the sublimity of the comprehensiveness of the truth of createdness, change and contingency; with the consensus of all scholars of the science of theology; with the testimony of the truth of the changing of its form and its contents, with wisdom and regularity, and the renewal of its letters and words with discipline and equilibrium; and with the testimony of the sublimity of the comprehensiveness of the truth of cooperation, mutual response and solidarity, reciprocal care, balance and protection, among all its beings, by witnessing and clear vision."

★ ★ ★

THEN THE ARDENT and inquisitive traveller, who was seeking the creator of the world, who had advanced through eighteen degrees and approached, at the end of an ascension to the throne of truth, a station where he was addressed directly with knowledge of the unseen, addressed his own spirit and said:

"In the noble opening sura of the Qur'an, the verses that extend from the beginning to the word *iyyaka* ("Thee alone") are like a form of praise and encomium uttered in the absence of the One praised; but the word *iyyaka* signifies a coming into His presence and addressing Him directly. So, too, we should abandon this seeking in absence and separation, and ask for the object of search from the object of our search. For one must ask the sun, that shows all things, concerning the sun, and that which shows all things, will show itself even more clearly. Just as we perceive and know the sun by its rays, so too we can strive to know our Creator, in accordance with our capacities, through His Beautiful Names and Sacred Attributes."

We will set forth here, with the utmost brevity and concision, two of the countless paths that lead to this goal; two of the infinite degrees of those two paths; and two of the abundant truths and details of those two degrees.

The first truth: there appears visible to our eye a comprehensive, permanent, orderly and awesome truth, one that changes, transforms and renews all beings in heaven and on earth, with imperious and incessant activity. Within the truth of that in every way wise activity, there is immediately perceived the truth of the manifestation of dominicality, and, in turn, within the truth of that in every way merciful manifestation of dominicality, is recognisable the truth of the epiphany of divinity.

From this continious, wise and imperious activity, the deeds of an All-Powerful and All-Knowing Doer can be discerned, as if from behind a veil. And from behind the veil of these nurturing and administering deeds of dominicality, the Divine Names, manifest in all things, can be immediately perceived. Then behind the veil of the Beautiful Names, manifest with splendor and beauty, can be deduced the existence and reality of the seven sacred attributes, with a degree of certain knowledge that is close to visual or even experiential certainty. Through the manifestation of these seven sacred attributes, according to the testimony of all creation, in a life-giving, powerful, knowledgeable, all-hearing, all-seeing, volitional and speech-endowed form, there appears to the eye of faith in the heart — inevitably, automatically and with full certainty — the existence of a Necessary Existent that is described by these attributes, a Unique One known by these names, a Peerless and Eternal Doer, in a form more evidential and brilliant than the sun. For a beautiful and profound book necessarily presupposes the act of writing; a well-built house presupposes the act of building. In turn, the acts of writing beautifully and building well presuppose the names of writer and builder, and the titles of writer and builder obviously imply the arts and attributes of writing and building. These arts and attributes presuppose a person, no doubt, who will be qualified by the names and attributes in question and exercise the arts in question. It is not possible for there to be a deed without a doer, or a name without one designated by the name; similarly, it is impossible for there to be an attribute without one qualified by that attribute, and for there to be a craft without a craftsman.

On the basis, then, of this truth and principle, the cosmos, with all the beings it contains, resembles a collection of profound books and letters written with the pen of fate, or countless buildings and palaces constructed with the hammer of God's power. Each part of the cosmos is, in a thousand different ways, the manifestation of the infinite deeds of the Compassionate Lord, and of the thousand and one Divine Names that are the source of those deeds. The Beautiful Names are in turn manifestations of their source, the seven attributes of transcendent glory; and finally those seven all-embracing and sacred attributes constitute countless indications and infinite proofs of the necessary existence in unity of the Possessor of Glory that is their source and whom they describe. So too all the beauty, goodness, value and perfection contained in all beings bear manifest witness to the beauty and perfection of the dominical deeds, the divine names, the eternal attributes, and the glorious qualities; they indicate too the sacred beauty and perfection of the most sacred Essence.

So the truth of dominicality that manifests itself in the truth of activity reveals and makes itself known in qualities and acts such as creating, originating, fashioning and bringing into being, with knowledge and wisdom; predetermining, forming, administering and changing with regularity and balance; transforming, causing to descend and perfecting, with purpose and will; and feeding, nurturing, and bestowing generosity and bounty, with tenderness and mercy. And within the truth of the manifestation of dominicality, the truth of the immediately perceived revelation of divinity makes itself known and recognized with the glorious and beauteous manifestations of the seven affirmative attributes: life, knowledge, power, will, hearing, sight and speech.

Just as the attribute of speech makes the Most Sacred Essence known through revelation and inspiration, so too the attribute of power makes the Essence known through its skilled works and effects, each of which is like a word assuming external shape. Presenting the cosmos from end to end under the aspect of an incarnate Book of Discernment, it describes and makes known a Powerful Possessor of Glory.

As for the attribute of knowledge, it makes known a single Most Sacred Essence, through each of the wise, well-ordered and symmetrical objects of creation, through each creature administered, directed, adorned and made distinct by God's knowledge.

As for the attribute of life, it is proven not only by its own evidences, but also by all the works that proclaim God's power, by all the well-ordered, wise, symmetrical and adorned forms and states that indicate God's knowledge, as well as all proofs of all other attributes. Thus life, pointing to all animate beings that act as mirrors reflecting those abundant proofs, makes known an Eternally Living and Self-Subsistent Essence.

It is also this attribute that constantly changes the cosmos, in order to produce in it ever fresh and various manifestations and designs, and turns it into a supreme mirror composed of countless smaller mirrors. Similarly, the attributes of seeing and hearing, willing and speaking, each reveal and make known the Most Sacred Essence, just as the cosmos does.

Then, too, just as the attributes point to the existence of the Possessor of Glory, they also indicate in most manifest fashion the existence and reality of life, and the livingness and permanence of that Essence. For knowing is a sign of life; hearing is an indication of life; seeing belongs only to the living; will takes place only with life. Purposive power is found only in the living, and speech is a task for those endowed with knowledge and life.

It follows from the foregoing that the attribute of life has proofs seven times as numerous as the cosmos, and evidences that proclaim its existence and the existence of the One Whom it qualifies. Thus it comes to be the foundation and source of all the attributes, the origin and support of the Supreme Name. Since the *Risale-i Nur* establishes this first truth with powerful proofs and clarifies it, we will content ourselves now with a drop from this ocean.

The second truth: divine discourse, that proceeds from the attribute of speech.

> "Were the sea to become ink for the words of my Lord...[21]"

According to the inner sense of this verse, divine discourse is infinite. The clearest sign demonstrating the existence of a being is his speech. This truth, therefore, constitutes an infinite testimony to the existence and unity of the Eternal Speaker. Since two powerful evidences of this truth are revelation and inspiration, set forth in the Fourteenth and Fifteenth Degrees of this treatise; another broad proof is provided by sacred and heavenly books, as indicated in the Tenth Degree; and a further most brilliant and comprehensive proof is furnished by the Qur'an of Miraculous Exposition, as discussed in the Seventeenth Degree — for all these reasons we refer our readers to those Degrees for the exposition and affirmation of this truth. Enough for us and our traveller, who was unable to proceed beyond this point, are the lights and mysteries contained in the sublime verse that proclaims this truth in miraculous fashion and adds

21. Qur'an 18:109

its own testimony to all of the preceding ones:

> "God bears witness that there is no god but
> He, as do the angels and the possessors
> of knowledge; steadfast in equity; there is no
> god but He, the Mighty, the Wise![22]"

In allusion to the core of the lesson learned by our traveller at this sacred station, we said, in the Nineteenth Degree of the First Station:

"There is no god but God, the Necessary Existent, the One, the Unique; His are the beautiful Names, His are the Supreme Attributes, and His is the Most Sublime Similitude. To His Necessary Existence in Unity points the necessarily existent Essence, with the consensus of all its sacred and comprehensive attributes and all of its beautiful names, manifest in all of His doings and deeds, by the testimony of the comprehensiveness of the truth of the self-revelation of divinity in the manifestation of dominicality, in the permanence of imperious activity through the act of bringing into being, creating, making and originating, in will and in power, and through the act of predestining, forming and administering, in choice and in wisdom; through the act of expending, preserving, ordering and maintaining, in purposiveness and mercy, in complete order and equilibrium; as too by the testimony of the sublimity of the comprehensiveness of the truth of the inward meanings of the verse:

22. Qur'an 3:18

"God bears witness that there is no god but
He, as do the angels and the possessors
of knowledge; steadfast in equity; there is no
god but He, the Mighty, the Wise![23]"

NOTE

Each of the truths that offer their testimony in
the Nineteen Degrees of the First Chapter of the
Second Station above, not only indicate Necessary
Existence through existence and presence, but
also, through their comprehensiveness, attest
God's oneness and unity. But since they prove
existence most clearly and explicitly, we regarded
them first as proofs of Necessary Existence.

As for the Second Chapter of the Second
Station, the truths in question will be designated
instead as proofs of unity, insofar as they explicitly prove unity, and implicitly necessity.
In reality, each proves the other: unity proves
necessity, and necessity proves unity. In order
to indicate the difference, we said repeatedly in
the First Chapter, "by the testimony of the sublimity of the comprehensiveness of the truth of...,"
while in the Second Chapter we shall recurrently
say, "by the witnessing of the sublimity of the
comprehensiveness of the truth of...," thus indicating the evident visibility of unity. I had the
intention of explaining the degrees of the Second

23. Qur'an 3:18

Chapter, just as I did in the First Chapter, but on account of various obstacles I am compelled to be summary and concise. I leave it to other parts of the *Risale-i Nur* to expound these matters as they deserve to be expounded.

★　★　★

SECOND CHAPTER

Concerning the proofs of the divine unity

THE TRAVELLER WHO had been sent to the world in order to attain faith, who journeyed through the whole cosmos in his mind in order to ask all things concerning their creator, to seek his Lord in every place and find his God, with the utmost certainty, at the point of Necessary Existence — this traveller said to his intellect: "Come, let us depart on a new journey in order to behold the proofs of the unity of our Necessarily Existent Creator."

They set off together. At the first stopping-place, they saw four sacred truths prevailing over the whole cosmos, truths that self-evidently necessitated the unity of God.

THE FIRST TRUTH: absolute divinity. The absorption of each class of men in a mode of worship dictated by their innate dispositions; the species of worship engaged in by other animate beings, as well as inanimate beings, through the performance of their essential functions; the way in which all material and moral bounties and gifts in the cosmos become means inciting men to worship and thanks, to praise and gratitude; the fashion in which all the manifestations of the unseen and the epiphanies of the spirit, revelation and inspiration, unanimously proclaim the exclusive fitness of one God to receive worship — all of this, in most evidential fashion, proves the reality and dominance of a single and absolute divinity. If the truth of such a divinity exists, it can in no way accept partnership. For those who respond to divinity — ie., the fitness to be worshipped — with thanks and worship, are the conscious and animate fruits on the highest branches of the tree of the cosmos. If others were able to gratify and place under their obligation those conscious beings in such fashion as to make them turn away from and forget their true object of worship — Who may, indeed, be swiftly forgotten, because of His invisibility — this would be in such utter contradiction to the essence of divinity and its sacred purposes that it could in no way be allowed. It is for this reason that the Qur'an so repeatedly and with such vehemence refutes polytheism and threatens the polytheists with Hellfire.

THE SECOND TRUTH: absolute dominicality.

The ubiquitous workings of a wise and merciful hidden hand throughout the cosmos, especially in animate beings and their nurturing and development, everywhere in the same fashion and yet in a totally unexpected form, must be, without doubt, the emanation and light of an absolute dominicality, and a decisive proof of its reality.

An absolute dominicality cannot accept any partnership. For since the important aims and purposes of dominicality, such as the manifestation of its beauty, the proclamation of its perfection, the revelation of its precious arts and the display of its hidden accomplishments, are combined and concentrated in particulars and animate beings, the slightest attribution to God of a partner, when entering even the most particular of things and the smallest of animate beings, will frustrate the attainment of those purposes, and destroy those aims. Averting the faces of conscious beings from those purposes and the One who conceived them toward causes, will be totally opposed and hostile to the essence of dominicality, and absolute dominicality cannot in any way countenance it.

The abundant proclamations in the Qur'an of God's sanctity and transcendence, its verses and words, even its letters and their shapes, are constant guides to God's unity, made necessary by the secret we have just expounded.

THE THIRD TRUTH: perfections.

The self-evident testimony to the existence of the truth of perfections given by all the exalted instances of wisdom in creation, all its wondrous beauties, its just laws, its wise purposes, and in particular its testimony to the perfections of the Creator, Who brought forth the cosmos out of the void and then administered it in every way miraculously and beauteously, as well as the perfections of man, who is the conscious mirror of the Creator — such testimony is extremely clear.

There exists, then, the truth of perfection, and the certainty that the Creator Who fashioned the cosmos in perfection must Himself possess perfection. Further, the perfections of man, the most important fruit of creation, God's viceregent on earth, the beloved and most valued object of His creation — these are also established as true. Therefore, to assign partners to God would be unacceptable and false, for it would condemn to destruction and perdition all of the perfect and wise beings we behold with our eyes; it would turn the cosmos into a vain plaything of accident, a place of amusement for nature, a cruel slaughterhouse for the animate, an awesome house of sorrows for the conscious; it would reduce man, whose perfections are visible in his works, to the level of the most wretched, distraught and vile animal; and it would draw a veil across the infinite perfections of the Creator that are reflected in the mirror of all beings, thus nullifying the result of His activity and denying His creativity.

Since the contradiction of assigning partners to God to divine, human and cosmic perfections and its denial of them has been established and explained in the First Station of the Second Ray (devoted to three fruits of the divine unity), with strong and decisive proofs, we refer our readers to that work and cut short the discussion here.

THE FOURTH TRUTH: Sovereignty.

Whoever looks at the cosmos with comprehensive attention, will see it to resemble a most prosperous and active kingdom, a city administered most wisely and ruled most firmly; he sees all things and all species obediently engaged in a particular function.

According to the military metaphor contained in the verse,

> "God's are the armies of the heavens and earth,[1]"

the wise commands, imperious orders and kingly laws enunciated in those numerous armies, that extend from the hosts of the atom, the battalions of the vegetable kingdom, the brigades of the animal kingdom, to the armies of the stars, and embrace both the lowliest soldier and the loftiest commander — they all indicate self-evidently the existence of an absolute sovereignty and a universal authority.

There is, then, a truth of absolute sovereignty, and there can be no truth of assigning partners to God. For according to the decisive truth of the verse,

> "were there to be in the heavens and earth gods other than God, verily they would be corrupted,[2]"

if numerous hands all engage assertively in the same task, the result will be confusion. If there are two kings in one country, or even two headmen in one district, order will disappear, and administration be replaced by anarchy. But on the

1. Qur'an 48:4
2. Qur'an 21:22

contrary we see everywhere such order, from the wing of the fly to the lamps of the heavens, from the cells of the body to the signs of the planets, that there is no possibility for the intervention of any partner in God's affairs.

Sovereignty is, moreover, a station of dignity; to accept a rival would flout the dignity of sovereignty. The fact that man, who needs the assistance of many people on account of his impotence, will kill his brothers and offspring in the cruellest fashion for the sake of some petty, apparent and temporary sovereignty, shows that sovereignty rejects all notion of partnership. If so feeble a one acts thus for the sake of so petty a sovereignty, it follows that the Possessor of Absolute Power, the Master of all creation, will never permit one other than Himself to participate in His sacred sovereignty, the fundament of His real and universal dominicality and divinity.

Since this truth has been established with firm proofs as numerous places throughout the *Risale-i Nur* and especially the Second Station of the Second Ray, we refer the reader to those pages for further discussion of it.

Through witnessing these four truths, our traveller came to know the divine unity with the degree of certain and clear witnessing. His faith shone, and with all his power he said, "there is no god but God, alone and without partner." In brief allusion to the lesson he derived from this station, we said, in the second Chapter of the First Station:

"There is no god but God, the One, the Unique, to Whose unicity* and the necessity of Whose being points the witnessing of the sublimity of the truth of the manifestation of absolute divinity, as well as the witnessing of the sublimity of the comprehensiveness of the truth of the manifestation of absolute dominicality that requires unity, the witnessing of the sublimity of the comprehensiveness of the truth of the perfections that arise from unity, and the witnessing of the sublimity of the comprehensiveness of the truth of absolute sovereignty, that prevents and contradicts the existence of any partnership."

★ ★ ★

THEN THAT RESTLESS traveller addressed his heart and said: "The fact that the people of faith, and particularly those affiliated with a Sufi order, are constantly repeating the words, 'no god but He,' and recalling and proclaiming God's unity, is an indication that the affirmation of God's unity comprises many degrees. Such affirmation is, moreover, a most enjoyable, most valuable and most exalted sacred duty, instinctive function and act of worship. Let us, then, in order to attain a further degree, open the door of another stopping-place in this abode of instruction. For

*Unity: God's uniqueness, the oneness of His essence. Unicity: oneness within multiplicity; the oneness and harmony of purpose joining together His numerous different attributes and acts (Trans).

the true affirmation of God's unity we seek is not some imaginary species of knowledge. It is rather an affirmation that in terms of logic is deemed the opposite of imagination, that is far more valuable than cognition based on imagination, that is the result of proof, that is designated as knowledge."

The true affirmation of God's unity is a judgement, a confirmation, an assent and acceptance that can find its Lord present with all things, that sees in all things a path leading to its Lord, and does not regard anything as an obstacle to His presence. For otherwise it would always be necessary to tear and cast aside the veil of the cosmos in order to find its Creator. "Onward, then," said the traveller to himself, as he knocked at the door of God's splendor and sublimity. He entered the stopping-place of God's deeds and workings, the world of creation and origination, and there he saw that five comprehensive truths were prevailing over the entire cosmos, and offering self-evident proof of the divine unity.

THE FIRST TRUTH: that of splendor and sublimity. Since this truth is explained with different proofs in the Second Station of the Second Ray, and various other places in the *Risale-i Nur,* we restrict ourselves here to the following:

The being that creates and then administers at a single time and in a single fashion the stars that are thousands of years distant from each other; that creates at a single time and in a single form the countless members of the same species of flower, distributed over the east and the west, the north and the south of the globe; that administers, nurtures, quickens, distinguishes and adorns more than two hundred thousand different types of plant and species of animal in five or six weeks, with the utmost regularity and equilibrium, without any confusion, defect or error, in order to provide every spring on the face of the earth more than a hundred thousand specimens of the supreme resurrection, and thus prove before man's eyes a remarkable event, now belonging to the past and the realm of the unseen, namely the creation of the heavens and the earth in six days, as indicated in the verse,

> "He it is Who created the heavens and the the earth in six days;[3]"

the being that causes the earth to revolve, as evidenced in the verse,

> "He merges night with day, and day with night,[4]"

and turns the night into the pages on which the events of the day are written — this same being knows and administers according to His own will, all at the same time, the most secret and obscure thoughts that occur to men's hearts. Since all of the aforementioned acts are in reality one act, it follows that their glorious Doer is a Unique and All-Powerful being, enjoying such

3. Qur'an 57:4
4. Qur'an 3:27

splendor and sublimity that nowhere, in nothing, in no way, does it leave the slightest possibility for the acceptance of partnership; on the contrary, it uproots all such possibility.

God possesses, then, such splendor and sublimity of power. His splendor is at the apex of perfection and comprehensiveness. It is therefore fully impossible that He should permit or leave the way open for the acceptance of partners to inflict need or impotence on His power, to induce deficiency in His splendor, to impose limitations on His comprehensiveness, to set a limit to His limitlessness. No sound intellect could deem this possible.

The assignment of partners to God is, then, by virtue of the offense it causes to God's splendor, the dignity of His magnificence and His sublimity, so grave a crime that the Qur'an of Miraculous Exposition decrees with an earnest threat,

> "God does not pardon the assignment to Him of a partner; He pardons whatever is lesser than that."

THE SECOND TRUTH: the absoluteness, the comprehensiveness and appearance in infinite form of the dominical deeds seen at work in the cosmos. It is only God's wisdom and will that limits and defines those deeds, as well as the inherent capacities of the objects and places in which they manifest themselves. Stray chance,

5. Qur'an 4:48

dumb nature, blind force, unconscious causality and the elements that without restriction are scattered in every direction — none of these can have any part in the most balanced, wise, perspicacious, life-giving, orderly and firm deeds of the Creator. They are used, rather, by the command, will and power of the Glorious Doer as an apparent veil to conceal His power.

Three out of innumerable examples:

We will set forth three from among the numerous subtle points that relate to the three deeds indicated in three continuous verses in *Surat an-Nahl.*

THE FIRST:

> "Thy Lord inspired in the bee that it should seek a dwelling-place in the mountains.[6]"

The bee is, with respect to its disposition and function, such a miracle of God's power that a whole sura, *Surat an-Nahl,* has been named after it. For to inscribe in the minute head of that little honey machine a complete program for the fulfilment of its important task; to place in its diminutive stomach the most delicious of foods and to ripen them there; to place in its sting poison capable of destroying and killing animate beings, without causing any harm to its own body or the member in question — to do all this with the utmost care and knowledge, with exceeding wisdom and purposiveness, partakes of a perfect orderliness and equilibrium, and hence unconscious, dis-

6. Qur'an 16:68

orderly, disequilibriated nature and accident could never interfere or participate in any of this.

The appearance and comprehensiveness of this divine craft, this dominical deed, which is miraculous in three separate respects, in the countless bees that are found scattered over the earth, with the same wisdom, the same care, the same symmetry, at the same time and in the same fashion — this is a self-evident proof of God's unity.

THE SECOND VERSE:

> "There is for you a lesson in cattle. From what is within their bodies, between excretions and blood, we produce, for your drink, milk, pure and agreeable to those who drink it."'

This verse is a decree overflowing with useful instruction. To place in the nipples of cows, camels, goats and sheep, as well as human mothers, in the midst of blood and excrement but without being polluted by them, a substance the exact opposite, pure, clean, pleasant, nutritive and white milk, and to inspire in their hearts tenderness toward their young that is still more pleasant, sweeter and more valuable than milk — this requires such a degree of mercy, wisdom, knowledge, power, will and care that it cannot in any way be the work of turbulent chance, of the tangled elements, or of blind forces.

The manifestation, workings and comprehensiveness of so miraculous a dominical art and so wise a divine deed, all over the face of the globe

7. Qur'an 16:66

and in the countless hearts and breasts of innumerable mothers of hundreds of thousands of species, in the same instant, the same fashion, with the same wisdom and the same care — this too constitutes a self-evident proof of God's unity.

THE THIRD VERSE:

"From the fruits of the date-palm and the vine ye take sugar and fine nourishment; verily therein is a sign for a people possessing intelligence.[8]"

This verse invites our attention to the date and to grapes, saying, "for those of intelligence, there is great proof, argument and evidence of the divine unity in these two fruits. These two fruits yield nurture and sustenance, fresh and dry fruit, and give rise to most delicious forms of food; yet the trees that bear them stand in waterless sand and dry soil, and are thus miracles of power and wonders of wisdom. They are each of them like a factory producing sweet sugar, a machine manufacturing honeylike syrup, a work of art created with perfect regularity, wisdom and care; hence anyone with a grain of intelligence will say on contemplating them, "the one who made them in this fashion may very well be the creator of the whole cosmos."

For in front of our eyes each finger-long vine branch will hold twenty branches of grapes, and each branch will in turn contain hundreds of

8. Qur'an 16:67

sugary grapes, each like a little pump emitting syrup. To clothe the surface of each grape with a fine, delicate, thin and colorful protection; to place in its delicate and soft heart seeds with their hard shells, which are in reality the means for its protection, the program and story of its life; to manufacture in its stomach a sweetmeat like the helva of Paradise, a honey like the water of Kauthar; to create an infinite number of such grapes over the face of the entire earth, with the same care and wisdom, and at the same time and in the same fashion — this proves in self-evident fashion that the one who fulfills these tasks is the Creator of the whole cosmos, and this deed, requiring as it does infinite power and limitless wisdom, can be only His deed.

Yes, blind and stray, disorderly and unconscious, aimless, aggressive and anarchic forces, nature and causality, cannot have anything to do with this most sensitive balance, this most skillful art, this most wise scheme. They cannot even stretch out their hands toward it. It falls to them only to be employed as passive objects, as curtain-holders and servants of God's command.

Just like the three points proving divine unity contained in the three truths indicated in the three verses, the countless manifestations and workings of infinite dominical deeds attest unanimously the unity of a unique and One, the Glorious Essence.

THIRD TRUTH: the creation of beings, particularly plants and animals, with absolute speed and absolute orderliness; with absolute ease and extreme skill, talent, ability, and order; with great value and distinction despite extreme frequency and commonness.

Yes, to produce with extreme swiftness and in extreme abundance, most skillfully and artistically, with great ease and facility combined with the utmost care and orderliness, with great value and distinction despite frequency and commonness, without any form of confusion or deficiency — this can be achieved only by a Unique Being Whose power is such that nothing appears difficult to it.

For that power it is as easy to create stars as atoms, the greatest as the smallest, a whole species as a single member of a species, a sublime and comprehensive universal as a restricted and petty particular; it is as easy for Him to revivify and quicken the whole earth as to do the same with a tree, or to erect a tree as tall as a mountain as it is to produce a seed no bigger than a fingernail. All of these deeds He performs in front of our eyes.

So the exposition, the solution, the uncovering and the proof of the mystery of this degree of the assertion of the divine unity, this third truth, this word of unity — the mystery that the greatest universal is like the smallest particular without the slightest difference between them — this beneficial wisdom, this supreme talisman, this riddle beyond the reach of the intellect, this most significant foundation of Islam, this most profound source of faith, this greatest fundament of the divine unity — the setting forth of all this opens the talisman of the Qur'an, and makes it possible to know the most secret and unknowable riddle of the creation of all beings, a riddle that reduces philosophy to impotence.

Thanks and praise one hundred thousand times the letters of the *Risale-i Nur* be to the Merciful Creator that the *Risale-i Nur* has solved, uncovered and established this wondrous talisman, this wondrous riddle. It has been proven with decisive arguments, to the same degree of certainty that twice two is four, particularly in the discussion of "He is powerful over all things" toward the end of the Twentieth Letter; in the section concerning God's being an all-powerful agent in the Twenty-Ninth Word, one devoted to the resurrection; and in the section proving the divine power in the degrees of "God is the greatest" in the Twenty-Ninth Flash, written in Arabic. For that reason we assign to those parts of the *Risale-i Nur* the exposition of this matter, wishing, however, to set out briefly the foundations and proofs that solve this mystery and to allude to thirteen mysteries that resemble thirteen steps, or a list of contents. I have indeed written the first and second mysteries, but unfortunately two powerful obstacles, moral and material, have caused me to abandon the remainder.

THE FIRST MYSTERY: if something be essential, its opposite cannot have access to the essence defined by that thing. For that would be equivalent to the union of opposites, which is an absurdity. Now with regard to this principle, since God's power is related to His Essence and is an essential concomitant of His Most Sacred Essence, impo-

tence — the opposite of power — cannot in any
way gain access to that All-Powerful Essence.

Moreover, the existence of degrees within a thing
comes about through the intervention in it of its
opposite. For example, strong and weak degrees
of light result from the intervention of darkness;
high and low degrees of heat proceed from the
admixture of coldness; and greater and lesser
amounts of strength are determined by the intervention and opposition of resistance. It is therefore impossible that degrees should exist in that
power of the Divine Essence. He creates all things
as if they were but a single thing. And since
degrees do not exist in the power of the divine
essence and it does not admit of weakness or deficiency, no obstacle can in any way obstruct it
nor can the creation of anything cause it difficulty.

Since, then, nothing is difficult for God's
power, He creates the supreme resurrection with
the same ease as spring; spring with the same
facility as a tree; and a tree with as little trouble
as a flower. Further, He creates a flower as
artistically as a tree; a tree as miraculously as a
spring; and a spring as comprehensively and
wondrously as a resurrection. All of this He ac-
complishes in front of our eyes.

It has been proved in the *Risale-i Nur* with
decisive and strong proofs that if there were no
divine unity and unicity, the making of a flower
would be as difficult as a tree or even more difficult; the making of a tree would be as hard as a
spring or even more difficult; and creation would
even lose its value and artistic quality. An animate

being that now takes a minute to produce would be produced with difficulty in one year, or maybe never at all.

It is, then, on account of this mystery that these fruits, flowers, trees and animals, that are extremely valuable despite their ubiquitousness and abundance, and extremely artistic despite the swiftness and ease of their fashioning, emerge in regular fashion onto the plain of being and assume their functions. Proclaiming God's glory, they accomplish their duties and depart, leaving behind their seed in their stead.

SECOND MYSTERY: through the mystery of luminosity, transparency and obedience, just as a single sun is reflected in one or more mirrors, so too a single manifestation of the power of God's Essence, an infinite power, bestows the same luminous and warm reflection on innumerable mirrors, shining objects and drops of water, through its extensive activity and God's command. Small and great are as one for it, and it makes no distinction between them.

So too if God utters one word, on account of His surpassing creativity and its surpassing comprehensiveness, it will enter, by God's leave, the ears of millions with the same ease that it enters the ears of one man. One listener is equivalent to thousands; there is no difference between them.

Then again a single light like the eye, a single spirit being like Gabriel, on account of the perfect comprehensiveness of the dominical activity contained within the manifestation of compassion, will be found in, will resort to, will regard thousands of different loci with the same ease that it is found in, resorts to and regards a single locus —this, by virtue of God's power. There is no difference here between the few and the many.

The pre-eternal power of God's essence is the most subtle and choicest of lights, the light of all lights; the quiddities, essences and inner dimensions of all things are luminous and lustrous as mirrors; all things, from the atom, the plant, and the animate creature to the stars, the suns and the moons, are extremely obedient and submissive to the command of that power of the Divine Essence and subordinate to the orders of that pre-eternal power. It is for all of these reasons entirely natural that innumerable things should be created with the same ease as a single thing and placed side by side with each other. No concern or task interferes with another. Great and small, many and few, particular and universal — all are the same for that power, for which nothing is difficult.

As was said in the Tenth and Twenty-Ninth Words, through the mysteries of order, equilibrium, obedience to command and submission to order, that power causes a great ship as big as a hundred houses, to move and advance as a child's finger pushes his toy.

As a commander will send a single infantryman into battle with an order from his throne, so too he may throw a whole obedient army into the fray with the same single order.

Let us suppose that two mountains are in a state of equilibrium in a large and sensitive balance. In the same way that a single walnut would cause one pan to rise and the other to fall if placed on one side of a balance containing two eggs, it would produce the same result with the scale containing the mountains; through a wise law it would cause one pan with its mountain to rise to the mountain top, and the other to descend with its mountain to the bottom of the valley.

Since there is to be found in God's absolute, infinite, luminous, essential and eternal power a divine justice and unending wisdom that is the origin, source, fundament and beginning of all order, regularity and equilibrium in creation; and since all things, particular and universal, small and great, are obedient to the command of that power and submissive to its workings — it follows that God causes the stars to revolve and to move, through the wisdom of His order, as easily as He rotates and moves the atoms.

In spring, just as He brings to life a single fly with a single order, so too He bestows life with the same ease and the same command on the whole species of fly, as well as all the hosts of plants and animals, through the mystery of the wisdom and equilibrium inherent in His power, and then sends them forth onto the plain of life.

In the same way that He swiftly gives life to a tree in spring and infuses vitality in its bones, with His wise and just absolute power, He also resurrects in the spring the corpse of the vast earth and brings into being hundreds of thousands of different specimens of resurrection similar to the tree, all this with the greatest of ease.

With His cosmic command, He brings the earth back to life. By the decree of

> "there will be but a single cry, then they shall all be brought nigh unto us[9],"

all men and jinn, with a single cry and command shall be brought to us and made present at the plain of resurrection. Again, by His command,

> "the hour shall be but a blinking of the eye, or even closer;[10]"

that is, the bringing about of resurrection and the gathering that follows upon it shall take no longer than the opening and closing of an eye, or even less. Then there is the verse,

> "your creation and resurrection is as a single soul,[11]"

meaning the following: "O men! To create you and to bring you to life, to resurrect and gather you, is as easy for me as bringing one soul to life; it presents no problem to My power." According to the inner sense of these three verses, God will bring all men and jinn, all animals, spirit beings and angels to the field of the supreme gathering and the great balance with a single command and with great ease. One concern does not interfere with another.

9. Qur'an 36:53
10. Qur'an 16:77
11. Qur'an 31:28

The remaining mysteries, from third and fourth as far as the thirteenth, have been postponed to another time in a fashion disagreeable to me.

FOURTH TRUTH: the existence and appearance of all beings proclaim the divine unity in a self-evident fashion through their numerous points of unity and convergence, such as being simultaneously together and yet separate and unique; being the miniature or magnified versions of each other; being some, universals and species, and some, particulars and individuals; resembling each other in the stamp of innate disposition; having affinity in the impress of artistry; and aiding and complementing each other with respect to their innate functions. They establish the oneness of their Maker, and with respect to the dominicality manifest in creation, they prove that there exists a universal being impervious to division and separation.

For example, in each spring, to create, order and sustain the innumerable members of the four hundred thousand different species of plants and animals, together and intermingled, in a single moment and in the same fashion, without any error or mistake, with the utmost wisdom and perfection of artistry; to create all the different species of bird, from flies, which are like birds in miniature, to eagles which are the supreme specimens of the species, then to equip them with the means of flight and subsistence and to cause them to journey through the realm of the air; to imprint on the countenances of each of the birds in miraculous fashion a stamp of artistry, on the body of each of them a seal of wisdom, and in the quiddity of each of them, in sustaining fashion, a sign of God's unity; to cause wisely and mercifully particles of food to hasten to the aid of the cells of the body, plants to rush to the assistance of animals, and all mothers to go swiftly to the help of their powerless infants; to work on all things, particular and universal, from the Milky Way, the solar system and the elements of the earth, down to the veils of the pupil of the eye, the petals of the rose, the husk of the corn, the seeds of the melon, like a series of intersecting circles, with the same regularity, perfection of artistry, the same single deed and plenitude of wisdom — to do all this establishes the following with the self-evident certainty:

He who performs these deeds is one and unique; His imprint is on all things. In the same way that He is not in any place, He is present in every place. Like the sun, all things are distant from Him, but He is close to all things. Just as the greatest objects, such as the Milky Way and the solar system, are not difficult for Him, so too the cells in man's blood and the thoughts that pass across his heart are not secret from Him nor beyond the reach of His power.

However great and multitudinous a thing may be, it is as easy for Him as the smallest and scarcest thing, for He creates with ease a fly on the model of an eagle, a seed in the form of a tree, a tree in the shape of a garden, a garden with the artistry of a spring, and a spring on the scale of a resurrection. Things most valuable in their artistry He gives to us and bestows upon us most cheaply. The price that He asks us is merely to say ''in the name of God'' and ''praise be to God.'' In other words, the accepted price for all those numerous precious bounties is to say at the beginning of all things, ''in the name of God, the Compassionate, the Merciful'' and at their end, ''praise be to God.''

Since this Fourth Truth is explained and expounded elsewhere in the *Risale-i Nur*, we content ourselves here with this brief allusion.

THE FIFTH TRUTH perceived by our traveller at the second stage: the existence in the entirety of the cosmos, its pillars and parts and all the beings contained in it, of the most perfect order and regularity; the uniqueness of the substances and purposive beings that are the means for the rotation and administration of that vast kingdom and are connected to its general scheme; the fact that the divine names and deeds that are at work in that magnificent city, that vast plain, encompass and comprehend all things or most things despite their interconnection and being each the same name and deed in every place; the fact that the elements and species that are the means for the administration, entertainment and construction of that well-adorned palace, cover the whole face of the earth in their diffusion, despite their interconnection, their each possessing a separate quiddity and their each being present everywhere as the same element and species — all of this demands, proves and affirms, necessarily and self-evidently, the following:

The Maker and Disposer of this cosmos, the Monarch and Nurturer of this realm, the Master and Builder of this palace, is one, unique, sole. He has neither like nor peer, neither minister nor aide. He has neither partner nor opposite, He has neither inability nor deficiency. Yes, order is in itself a perfect expression of unity; it demands a single orderer. It leaves no place for the assignment of partners to God, the source of dispute and dissension.

There is a wise and precise order inherent in all things, whether universal or particular, from the total scheme of the cosmos and the daily and annual rotation of the earth down to the physiognomy of man, the complex of senses in man's head and the circulation of white and red cells in man's blood. Nothing other than One Absolutely Powerful and Absolutely Wise can stretch out its hand purposively and creatively toward any thing, nor interfere with it. On the contrary, all things are recipients, means of manifestation, and passive.

Now ordering, the pursuit of certain purposes and the bestowal of regularity with a view to certain benefits, can be done only by means of knowledge and wisdom and performed only with will and choice.

Certainly and in all events, this wisdom-nurturing regularity, this infinitely varied ordering of the cosmos that before our very eyes assures various benefits, proves and affirms to a self-evident degree that the Creator and Disposer of all beings is one, an agent possessing will and choice. Everything comes into being through His power, assumes a particular state through His will, and takes on a particular form through His choice.

The heat-giving lamp of this hospice that is the world is one; its candle that is the basis for the reckoning of time is one; its merciful lance is one; its fiery cook is one; its life-giving beverage is one; its well-guarded field is one, as well as a thousand and one other instances of oneness. It follows from all of these instances of oneness that the Maker and Master of this hospice is also one, that He is extremely generous and hospitable, for He employs numerous high-ranking and great officials to serve the animate guests of His hospice.

Names such as All-Wise, Merciful, Giver of of Forms, Disposer, Quickener, and Nurturer, the impresses and manifestations of which are to be seen at work in every corner of the world, attributes such as wisdom, mercy and grace, and acts such as formation, disposition and nurturing, are all one. They embrace every place in the utmost degree, each name and act being present there.

They also complement the imprint of each other in such a way that it is as if those names and deeds were uniting in such fashion that power becomes identical with wisdom and mercy, and wisdom becomes identical with grace and life.

For example, as soon as the activity of the name Quickener appears in a thing, the activity of numerous other names such as Creator, Giver of Forms, and Provider, also appears in the same measure. This of a certainty and self-evidently establishes and proves that that which is designated by the names and the doer of the comprehensive deeds that appear everywhere in the same fashion must also be one, single and unique. In this we believe and to this we give our assent!

The elements that are the substance and material of creation encompass the whole earth. Each of the species of creation that bears an imprint attesting unity is diffused throughout the earth in unity and, so to speak, conquers it. This also proves to the degree of being self-evident that those elements, together with what they embrace, and those species, together with their separate members, are the product and property of a single being. They are the products and servants of so Unique and Powerful a One that He employs those vast and imperious elements as obedient servants and those species diffused throughout the earth as well-disciplined soldiers. Since this truth also has been established and explained at other places in the *Risale-i Nur*, we content ourselves here with this brief indication.

In summary of the witnessings that he derived from these five truths, through the superabundance of faith and the joy of divine unity, and in expression of his feelings, our traveller said to his heart:

Look upon the colored page of the cosmic book;
See what forms the golden pen of power has traced.

*No dark point remains for the gaze of
the heart's eye;
It is as if God has inscribed His signs
with Light.*

Know too that:
*The leaves in the world's book are dimensions
infinite;
The inscriptions of destiny are works
innumerable.
Written on the Preserved Tablet of
Truth,
Like a profound word, is every being in
this world.*

Listen also to this:

When all things proclaim, 'no god but God,' they will in unison say, 'o Truth and Reality!' and beseech in harmony, 'o Living One!' Yes, in all things there is a sign pointing to the fact that He is One.

Hearkening to this, his heart and soul affirmed the truth of what they heard and said, "yes, indeed!"

In brief allusion to the five truths of unity observed by our traveller through the world, our voyager through the cosmos, at this second stopping place, it was said in the Second Chapter of the First Station:

"There is no god but God, the One, the Unique, to Whose Unity in Necessary Existence points the witnessing of the truth of Splendor and Magnificence, in its perfection and comprehensive-

ness; the witnessing of the truth of the appearance
of deeds in absolute fashion, in infinitude, without
any limitation except that of God's will and
wisdom; the witnessing of the truth of the creation
of beings in absolute multiplicity with absolute
swiftness, the creation of creatures in absolute ease with absolute perfection, the origination of things made in absolute plenitude
with utter perfection of artistry and value;
the witnessing of the truth of the existence
of beings in universal and comprehensive fashion,
joined, interconnected and interrelated; the witnessing of the truth of universal order, an order
incompatible with the assignation of partners to
God; the witnessing of the oneness of the sources
of cosmic order, a oneness that clearly attests
the oneness of their Maker; the unity of the names
and deeds that comprehend and permeate the universe; and the unity of the elements and species
dispersed over the face of the earth in imperious
fashion.''

★   ★   ★

THAT WORLD TRAVELLER voyaging through different ages chanced upon the school of the Re-
newer of the Second Millenium, Imam-i Rabbani
Ahmad Faruqi. He entered and listened to the
lesson being taught by the Imam:

    "The most important result yielded by all the
Sufi paths is the unfolding of the truths of faith.

The unfolding in clarity of a single truth of the faith is preferable to a thousand miraculous deeds and mystical visions."

The Imam said too:

"In former times, great persons said that someone will arise from among the theologians and the scholars of the science of theology. He will prove all the truths of faith and Islam with rational proofs and the utmost clarity. I wish to be that man and maybe I am.[12]"

He continued his instruction by saying that belief and the assertion of the divine unity were the foundation, substance, light and life of all human perfection; that the *hadith* "an hour's meditation is better than a year's worship" refers to meditation on faith; and that the silent mode of invocation practised in the Naqshbandi order is a form of this most excellent meditation.

The traveller listened with utmost care. He turned and addressed himself as follows: "It is thus that this heroic Imam speaks. To increase the strength of one's faith by as much as an atom is worth more than a ton of gnosis or other form of perfection and sweeter than the honey of a hundred visionary experiences.

"On the other hand, the philosophers of Europe have leagued together for more than a thousand years to invent objections and doubts in their

12. Time has proven that the man referred to here is not infact an individual, but the *Risale-i Nur* itself. It may be that the people of unveiling happened to notice the insignificant interpreter and proclaimer of the *Risale-i Nur* and hence came to speak of "a man".

hostility to faith and the Qur'an, and to attack the believers. They wish to shake the pillars of faith that are the key, the source, the foundation of everlasting felicity, of life immortal, of eternal paradise. We ought therefore to strengthen our faith by making it one of realization instead of one of imitation. So come, let us advance! In order to bring the twenty-nine degrees of faith that we have found, each as powerful as a mountain, to the blessed number of thirty-three, the number of the litanies that follow upon prayer, and in order to see a third stopping-place in this realm of instruction, let us knock at the door of the dominical sustenance of the animate world and open it with the key of 'in the name of God, the Compassionate, the Merciful,'" Speaking thus he beseechingly knocked at the gate of this third stopping-place, a compendium of wonders and a spectacle of marvels.

Saying, "in the name of God, the Opener," he opened the gate. The third stopping-place became visible to him. He entered and saw that it was illumined by four great and encompassing truths that demonstrated the divine unity as brightly as the sun.

THE FIRST TRUTH: the truth of opening. That is, the opening up from a single simple substance of innumerable varied and separate forms, together, everywhere, in a single instant and by a single deed, through the manifestation of the name Opener.

Yes, in the same way that God's creative power has opened up innumerable beings like flowers in the garden of the cosmos, and endowed each with an orderly form and distinct identity, through the manifestation of the name Opener, so too, although in more miraculous fashion, He has given to the four hundred thousand species of animate beings in the garden of the earth each its symmetrical, adorned and distinct form.

> "He creates you in the wombs of your mothers, creation after creation in three darknesses. That is God, your Lord. His is the kingdom; there is no god other than He. Where, then, wilt ye turn?[13]"

> "Nought is hidden from God, neither on earth nor in the heavens. He it is Who forms you in the wombs as he wills; there is no god but He, the Mighty, the Wise.[14]"

As these two verses indicate, the strongest proof of the divine unity and the most remarkable miracle of divine power is God's opening up of forms. Because the opening of forms is repeatedly established and expounded in different ways elsewhere in the *Risale-i Nur* and particularly in the Sixth and Seventh Degrees of the First Chapter of the Second Station of this treatise, we refer the discussion of this matter to those places and restrict ourselves here to the following:

According to the testimony of botany and biology, based on profound research, there is in the opening and unfolding of forms, such com-

13. Qur'an 39:6
14. Qur'an 3:5-6

prehensiveness and artistry that other than a Single and Unique One, One Absolutely Powerful, able to see and do all things in all things, no one could undertake this comprehensive and all-embracing deed. For this deed of the unfolding of forms demands a wisdom, an attention and a comprehensiveness that are present at all times and are contained within an infinite power. This power, in turn, can be found only in that Unique Being Who administers the whole cosmos.

As is decreed in the above-quoted verses, God's attribute of ''opening'' expressed in the opening and creation of the forms of men from their mothers' wombs, within three darknesses, separately, with equilibrium, distinctness, and order, without any error, confusion, or mistake; this truth of the unfolding of the forms of all men and animals, all over the earth, with the same power, the same wisdom and the same artistry, is a most powerful proof of God's unity. For to comprehend and embrace all things is itself a form of unity that leaves no room for the assignation of partners to God. Just as the nineteen truths of the First Chapter bearing witness to the necessary existence of God also attest the existence of the Creator through their own existence, so too they bear witness to the unity through their comprehensiveness.

THE SECOND TRUTH seen by our traveller in the third stopping-place: the truth of compassionateness. We see with our own eyes that there is one who has covered the face of the earth with thousands of gifts of compassion, and made it into a feasting-place. He has laid out a spread of hundreds of thousands of the different delicious foods of compassionateness, and made the inside of the earth a storehouse containing thousands of precious bounties of mercy and wisdom. That Being sends to us also the earth, in its yearly rotation, like a ship or a train, laden with the finest of the hundreds of thousands of vital human necessities, proceeding from the world of the unseen; and He sends to us too the spring, like a wagon carrying food and clothing for us. Thus does He nurture us, with utmost mercy. In order for us to profit from those gifts and bounties, He has moreover given us hundreds and thousands of appetites, needs, feelings, sensations and senses.

As was set forth in the Fourth Ray concerning the verse on the sufficiency of God, He has given us a stomach that can take pleasure in infinite varieties of food.

He has given us such a life that through the senses associated with it we can derive benefit from the innumerable bounties of the vast corporeal world, just as if it were some bounteous spread.

He has favored us with the human state so that we delight in the boundless gifts of both the spiritual and material worlds, through instruments such as the intellect and the heart.

He has conveyed Islam to us so that we derive light from the boundless treasuries of the unseen and manifest realms.

He has guided us to faith so that we are illumined by the innumerable lights and gifts of this world and the hereafter. This cosmos is like a palace fitted out and adorned by the divine quality of mercy with innumerable antiques and valuable items, which then gives to man's hands the keys to open all the chests and chambers in that palace, as well as bestowing on man's nature all the needs and senses that will enable him to make use of them.

This mercy that embraces this world and the hereafter, and indeed all things, is without doubt a manifestation of unicity within oneness.

Just as the light of the sun is a parable of unity, through its comprehending all things that face it, every bright and transparent object that receives the reflection of the light, heat and seven colors of the sun, is also a parable and a symbol of unity. Hence whoever sees its all embracing light will conclude that the sun of this earth is one and unique. Witnessing the warm and luminous reflection of the sun in all bright objects, and even in drops of water, he will say that the unity of the sun, or the sun itself, is present with its attributes close to all things; it is at the mirrorlike heart of all things.

So too the encompassing of all things by the extensive mercy of One Compassionate and Possessing of Beauty demonstrates the unicity of that Compassionate One. Similarly, the way in which that Compassionate One endows all things, particularly animate beings and more especially man, with a vital comprehensiveness that has regard for each individual and establishes a link among all things, as a manifestation of the lights of most of the names of the Compassionate One and His Essence — this also proves the Oneness of the Compassionate One and the fact that it is He Who does all things in all things.

Yes, the Compassionate One shows the splendor of His glory in the whole of the cosmos and all over the earth through the unity and comprehensiveness of His mercy. With the manifestation of His Unicity, He gathers together in every member of all animate species, and particularly man, specimens of all His bounties, orders the tools and instruments of animate beings, and proclaims the special solicitude of His beauty to each individual, this without shattering the unity of the cosmos. As for man, it is in him that God makes known in concentrated form the various forms of His bounty.

Similarly, a melon can be said to be concentrated within its seed; the Being that makes the seed must necessarily be He Who makes the melon. Then, with the special balance of His knowledge and the particular law of His wisdom, He draws the seed out from it, gathers it together and clothes it in a body. Nothing other than the one and unique master craftsman who makes the melon is able to make its seed. That would be impossible.

Since through the manifestation of Compassionateness the cosmos becomes like a tree or a garden, the earth becomes like a fruit or a melon, and man becomes like a seed, of a certainty the Creator and Lord of the smallest animate being must be the creator of all the earth and all the cosmos.

In short, just as the making and unfolding of the regular and orderly forms of all beings through the essence of the comprehensive attribute of Opener proves unity to the point of being self-evident, so too the essence of the comprehensive attribute of Compassionate, through its nurturing of all animate beings that come into existence and enter the life of this world, particularly the newly arrived, with the utmost order and regularity, its production of all necessary tools without any omission, and its reaching every individual at every place in every moment with the same mercy — this attribute too demonstrates both unicity and unity within unicity.

Since the *Risale-i Nur* is a manifestation of the name of All-Wise and the name of Merciful, and the various points and manifestations of the essence of mercy are explained and established in numerous places throughout the *Risale-i Nur*, we will be content here with this indication of a drop from the ocean, and cut short an extremely long story.

THE THIRD TRUTH witnessed by our traveller in the third stopping-place: the truth of disposing and administering. That is, to administer with complete order and equilibrium both the awesome and swift-moving heavenly bodies and imperious, interfering elements, and the needy, weak denizens of earth; to cause them to aid each other; to administer them jointly with each other; to take all necessary measures concerning them; and to make this vast world like a perfect kingdom, a magnificent city, a well-adorned palace.

Leaving aside the vast spheres of this imperious and compassionate administration, since it is explained and established in important sections of the *Risale-i Nur* such as the Tenth Word, we will show, by means of a metaphor, a single page and stage of that administration as it manifests itself in the spring on the face of the earth.

Let us suppose, for example, that some wondrous world conqueror assembled an army from four hundred thousand different groups and nationalities, and supplied the clothes and weapons, the instructions and dismissals and salaries of every group and nationality, separately and variously, without any defect or shortcoming, without error or mistake, at the proper time, without any delay or confusion, with the utmost regularity and in most perfect form, no cause other than the extraordinary power of that wondrous commander could stretch out its hand to attempt that vast, complex, subtle, balanced, multitudinous and just administration. Were it to stretch out its hand, it would destroy the equilibrium and cause confusion.

So too we see with our own eyes that an unseen hand creates and administers every spring a magnificent army composed of four hundred thousant different species. In fall — a specimen of the day of resurrection — three hundred thousand out of those four hundred thousand species of plants and animals are dismissed from their duties and go on leave, through the activity of death and in the name of decease.

In spring — a specimen of the gathering that

follows resurrection — three hundred thousand examples of raising from the dead are caused to arise in the space of a few weeks, with the utmost order and discipline. In the case of the tree, three such risings take place with respect to the tree itself, its leaves, its flowers and its fruits. Spring is shown to our eyes exactly like the preceding one, and each species and group in that army of glory that contains four hundred thousand different species is given its appropriate sustenance and provision, its defensive weapons and distinctive garments, its orders and dismissals, and all the tools and instruments it needs, with the utmost order and regularity, without error or slip, without confusion or omission, in unexpected fashion and at the proper time. This establishes within the perfection of dominicality, sovereignty and wisdom, unity, unicity and uniqueness, and writes the decree of God's unity on the face of the earth, on every page of spring, with the pen of destiny.

After reading a single page of this vernal decree, our traveller addressed his own soul saying:

"The torment of hellfire is pure justice for those who commit the error of denying resurrection. For such denial would be to refute the numerous promises and to deny the power of One Powerful and Almighty, One Wrathful and Possessing Splendor, Who has promised and assured all of His prophets thousands of times and set forth in thousands of verses of the Qur'an, explicitly and by way of allusion, that He will bring about a resurrection and gathering far easier for Him than the thousands of miraculous gatherings that occur every spring, each more wondrous than the Supreme Gathering.'' His soul responded: ''We believe in what you say.''

THE FOURTH TRUTH witnessed by the traveller through the world (the Thirty-Third Degree): the truth of Mercifulness and Bestowal of Provision. That is, the giving, over the whole face of the globe, within the earth, in the air above it and the ocean around it, to all animate beings, especially those endowed with spirit, and among them especially the impotent, the weak and the young, all of their necessary sustenance, moral and material, in the most solicitous manner, deriving it from dry and crude soil, from solid, bonelike dry pieces of wood, and in the case of the most delicate of all forms of sustenance, from between blood and urine, at the proper time, in orderly fashion, without any omission or confusion, in front of our eyes, by a hand from the unseen.

Yes, the verse

> ''God is the provider, the firm possessor of strength,[15]''

restricts to God the task of sustaining and providing, and the verse,

> ''there is no moving thing on earth but depends on God for its sustenance; it knows its resting-place and storage-place; all is in a book perspicuous,[16]''

15. Qur'an 51:58
16. Qur'an 11:6

provides a dominical guarantee and pledge to furnish provision for all men and animals. Similarly, the verse,

> "the beasts do not carry their sustenance; God sustains them and you, and He is All-Hearing, All-Knowing,[17]"

establishes and proclaims that it is God Who guarantees and provides for all impotent, powerless, weak and wretched creatures that are unable to secure their own sustenance, in an unexpected fashion, indeed from the unseen or even from nowhere; it is He for example Who provides for insects on the ocean bed and their young. This proclamation is directed in particular to those men who worship causes and are unaware that it is He who bestows provision from behind the veil of causality. Numerous other verses of the Qur'an and innumerable pieces of cosmic evidence unanimously demonstrate that it is the mercy of a single Glorious Provider that nurtures all animate beings.

Now the trees require a certain form of sustenance but have neither power nor will. They remain therefore in their places, trusting in God, and their provision comes hastening to them. So too the sustenance of infants flows to their mouths from wondrous small pumps, aided by the solicitude and tenderness of their mothers, for it could otherwise be severed by the exercise of will and power. These various

17. Qur'an 29:60

instances clearly prove that licit sustenance is not the result of will and power, but rather of the weakness and impotence that are induced by trusting in God.

Will, power and cleverness frequently incite greed, which is a source of loss, and often push certain learned men toward a form of beggary, whereas by contrast the trusting weakness of the boorish, crude and common man may cause him to attain riches.

The proverb, "how many a learned man has striven in vain, and how many an ignoramus gained rich provision," establishes that licit provision is not won by power and will, but by a mercy that finds working and striving acceptable; it is bestowed by a tenderness that takes pity on need.

Now provision and sustenance is of two kinds:

The first is true and innate provision, that required for life; this is guaranteed by the Lord. It is indeed so regular and well-ordered that this innate provision, stored in the body in the form of fat and other things, is enough to ensure survival for at least twenty days, even if nothing is eaten. Those who apparently die of hunger before the twenty or thirty days are up and before the provision stored up in their body is exhausted, die in reality not from lack of provision, but from a disease arising from lack of caution and the disturbance of fixed habit.

The second form of provision: metaphorical and artificial provision, arising from habit, wastefulness and misuse, but acquiring the appearance of necessity. This form is not guaranteed by the Lord, but depends on His generosity: sometimes He may give it, sometimes He may not give it. With respect to this second form of provision and sustenance, happy is he who regards his frugality — a source of happiness and pleasure — contentment and licit striving, as a form of worship and active prayer for sustenance. He accepts God's bounty gratefully and appreciatively, and passes his life in happy fashion.

Wretched is he who on account of prodigality — the source of wretchedness and loss — and greed, abandons licit striving, knocks at every door, passes his life in sloth, oppression and wretchedness, and indeed puts his own life to death.

In the same way that a stomach requires sustenance, so too the subtle capacities and senses of man, his heart, spirit, intelligence, eye, ear and mouth, also request their sustenance from the Merciful Provider and gratefully receive it. To each of them separately and in appropriate form is presented such provision from the treasury of mercy as will rejoice them and give them pleasure. Indeed, the Merciful Provider, in order to give to them provision in more generous measure has created each of man's subtle capacities — eye and ear, heart, imagination and intellect — in the form of a key to His treasury of mercy. For example, the eye is a key to the treasury containing such precious jewels as the fairness and beauty to be seen on the face of creation, and the same holds true of all the others mentioned; they all benefit through faith. To resume after our digression:

The Powerful and Wise Being Who created this cosmos created also life as a comprehensive summary of the cosmos, and concentrated all of His purposes and the manifestations of His names therein. So too, within the realm of life, He made of provision a comprehensive center of activity and created within animate beings the taste for provision, thus causing animate beings to respond to His dominicality and love with a permanent and universal gratitude, thankfulness and worship that is one of the significant purposes and instances of wisdom inherent in the creation of the cosmos.

For example, it is one of the activities of dominicality to cause every area of the broad realm of dominicality to rejoice — the heavens are caused to rejoice with the angels and spirit beings, the world of the unseen with spirits, and the material world, particularly the air and the earth, with the existence of all animate beings, particularly birds, great and small, at all times and places. Through the wisdom of this causing to rejoice and the infusion of life and spirit, animals and men are, as it were, whipped by the need for provision and the pleasure they take therein to pursue their provision and sustenance, thus being delivered from sloth. This, too, is one of the wise activities of dominicality. Were it not for such significant instances of wisdom, the provision destined for animals would be caused instinctively to hasten toward them to satisfy their needs, without any effort on their part, just as provision and sustenance is caused to hasten toward the tree.

Were there to be an eye capable of witnessing and comprehending the whole surface of the earth at one time, in order to perceive the beauties of the names of Merciful and Provider and the witness they bear to Unicity, it would see what sweet beauty is contained in the tender and solicitous manifestation of the Merciful Provider Who sends to the caravans of animals at the end of winter, when their provision is about to be exhausted, extremely delicious, abundant and varied foods and bounties, drawn exclusively from His unseen treasury of mercy, as succor from the unseen and divine generosity, placed in the hands of the plants, the crowns of trees and the breasts of mothers. The possessor of that all-seeing eye would realise that:

The making of a single apple, and the generous giving of it to a man as true sustenance and provision, can be accomplished only by a Being Who causes the seasons, the nights and the days to rotate, Who causes the globe to revolve like a cargo ship, and thus brings the fruits of the seasons within reach of those needy guests of the earth who stand waiting for them. For the imprint of artistry, the seal of wisdom, the imprint of eternal-besoughtedness, the signet of mercy that is to be found on the surface of the apple, is to be found also on all apples and other fruits, plants and animals. Hence the true Master and Maker of the apple is bound to be the

Glorious Master and the Beauteous Creator of all the inhabitants of the world, who are the peers, the congeners and the brothers of the apple; of the vast earth that is the garden of the apple; of the tree of the cosmos that is its factory; of the seasons that are its workshop; and of the spring and summer that are its place of maturing.

In other words, every fruit is a seal of unity that demonstrates the existence and unity of the Writer and Maker of the earth and the book of the cosmos that are the tree and the garden where the fruit grows. The fruits provide manifold indication of the seal affixed to the decree of unity.

Since the *Risale-i Nur* is a manifestation of the names of Merciful and Wise, and numerous flashes and mysteries of the truth of Mercifulness have been expounded and established in many parts of the *Risale-i Nur*, we leave further discussion of the matter to those parts and content ourselves with this brief indication, out of a vast treasury, on account of the unfavorable circumstances from which we are now suffering.

Our traveller now says then: "Praise be to God! I have seen and heard Thirty-Three Truths bearing witness to the necessary existence and unity of the Creator and Sovereign I was everywhere seeking and enquiring after. Each of the truths is bright, and leaves no darkness behind. It is as strong and unshakeable as a mountain. Each of them, with its certainty, bears decisive witness to His existence, and with its comprensiveness proves His unity in manifest fashion. While proving implicitly all the pillars of faith, the

totality and consensus of these truths causes our
faith to advance from imitation to realization,
from realization to knowledge of certainty, from
knowledge of certainty to vision of certainty,
and from vision of certainty to identity with
certainty. Praise be to God; this is from the bounty
of my Lord."

> "Praise be to God Who guided us to this;
> verily we would not have been guided unless
> God had guided us. The messengers of God
> have come to us with the truth.[18]"

In extremely brief allusion to the lights of
faith derived by our inquisitive traveller from the
four sublime truths he witnessed at the third
stopping-place, it was said in the second chapter
of the First Station, concerning the truths of
the Third Stopping Place:

"There is no god other than God, the One, the
Unique, to Whose Unity in Necessary Existence
points the witnessing of the magnificence of the
comprehensiveness of the truth of opening,
through the unfolding of different forms of four
hundred thousand species of living beings, perfect
and without defect, according to the testimony
of biology and botany; the witnessing of the
magnificence of the comprehensiveness of the
truth of compassionateness, all-embracing and
regular, without any deficiency, as the eye can
see; the witnessing of the magnificence of the truth
of administering, that encompasses in orderly

18. Qur'an 7:43

fashion all living beings, without error or defect; the witnessing of the magnificence of the comprehensiveness of the truth of mercifulness and sustaining, embracing all consumers of sustenance, at every time of need, without any mistake or forgetfulness; glory be unto Him, the Provider, the Compassionate, the Merciful, the Solicitous, the Generous; His gifts are universal, and His Generosity is all-embracing; there is no god, but He. Glory be unto Thee; we have no knowledge save that which thou hast taught us; verily Thou art All-Knowing, All-Wise! O Lord, for the sake of "in the name of God, the Compassionate, the Merciful", O God, O Compassionate One, O Merciful One! Bestow peace and blessings upon our master Muhammad, his family and all his companions, to the number of all the letters in the *Risale-i Nur*, multiplied by ten times the number of minutes in all of our lives in this world and the hereafter, and then by the number of particles in my body throughout the course of my life. Forgive me, and those who aid me in sincerity in the copying and distribution of the *Risale-i Nur*, and our fathers, our masters, our shaykhs, our sisters, our brothers, and the sincere students of the *Risale-i Nur*, particularly those who write and copy this treatise; by Thy Mercy, O Most Merciful of the Merciful, Amen. The conclusion of our prayer is, 'Praise be to God, the Lord of the Worlds!' "

★ ★ ★

NOTE

Since the other parts of the *Risale-i Nur* were not available in the place that saw the composition of the foregoing treatise, which was of necessity written down here, certain important matters of other Words and the Flashes have been mentioned also in the Supreme Sign, in what is an apparent repetition. In order to have the students of the *Risale-i Nur* in this area write a complete *Risale-i Nur* in miniature, we nonetheless had them write down all the present treatise.

The revised copy of this rough draft was written by a certain blessed person. Even though he was ignorant of such matters, we saw in the copy prepared by him a subtle and profound correspondence of the letters: there were six hundred and sixty-six *alifs**written at the beginning of the lines in his copy. This number corresponds fully with the value according to the *abjad* of the title given to this treatise by Imam 'Ali (may God be pleased with him), *Ayat al-Kubra* (The Supreme Sign), and thus demonstrates the suitability of this title for the treatise. We also understood this numerical correspondence to be an indication that this treatise is a flash derived from the light of the verses of the Qur'an for they are six thousand six hundred and sixty-six in number.

Said Nursi

**Alif:* first letter of Arabic alphabet

On the Purpose of
the *Risale-i Nur*

Today, I listened to an imaginary exchange of question and answer. Let me set forth for you a summary of it.

Someone said: "The great mobilization and complete preparedness of the *Risale-i Nur* for the sake of belief and the proving of the divine unity is constantly increasing. One hundredth part of its contents is enough to silence the most obstinate atheist; why then this further feverish mobilization and preparation?"

They answered him: "The *Risale-i Nur* is not repairing some minor damage to some petty structure; rather it is repairing vast damage to an all-embracing castle that shelters Islam and the stones of which are each as large as a mountain. It is striving to reform not a private heart, an individual conscience; rather it is attempting to cure, by means of the miraculousness of the Qur'an and the remedies of faith, the collective heart and mind that has been awesomely subverted by tools of corruption that have been prepared and stored for thousands of years, and the general conscience that is facing destruction as

143

a result of the shattering of those Islamic foundations and creeds that are the refuge of all, particularly the believers. For such awesome and universal damage, shattering and wounds, proofs of the utmost certitude and the strength of mountains are needed, as well as well-proven remedies and countless drugs each with the property of a thousand electuaries. This function is fulfilled in our time by the *Risale-i Nur* which emerges from the miraculousness of the Qur'an of miraculous exposition and is also a means for advancing and progressing through the infinite degrees of belief.''

A long discussion ensued to which I listened, offering infinite thanks. I curtail the matter here.

Said Nursi

In Appreciation

This work is the work of a fiery intellect,
This is the genius awaited by all ages.
All of these lights are the superabundant
    lights of the world of humanity;
It is God's epiphany shining within these truths,
    have no doubt!
O master! All men are amazed at thy
    outpouring, amazed at thy light;
The intelligent who find their desire in thy
    work proclaim, "no fault can be found!"
Those who read these writings found a fresh
    new world of light, through God's favor;
It is without doubt God who creates waves
    of Light in men's hearts.

Your Student Husrev

In confirmation of the words of our brother
we say:
It is an obstacle to all doubt and temptation,
A source of amazement for all learning
    and philosophy.
To the eye of intelligence no point remains dark;
It is a source of grace and advancement.
It is a manifestation of the Path and the Truth;
To the eye of intelligence no point now
    remains dark.

Students of the *Risale-i Nur,*
Tahiri, Zubeyr, Ceylan, Bayram
Abdulmuhsin

Question and Answer

It is fitting to record here an important answer given to a highly important question. For in this lesson the Old Said speaks as if forty years ago he had foreseen the wondrous lessons and effects of the *Risale-i Nur*. We shall therefore write down here the question and answer.

Many people have asked both myself and the students of *Risale-i Nur* the following question: "Why is it that the *Risale-i Nur* has not been defeated by so many opponents, obstinate philosophers and the people of misguidance? They have been able, to a degree, to prevent the dissemination of millions of true and valuable books concerning faith and Islam; they have deprived of the truths of faith numerous wretched youths and men addicted to vice and the pleasures of worldly life; and they have striven to break the *Risale-i Nur*, make men abandon it and shy away from it, through violent attacks, treacherous conduct, and lying propaganda. But the *Risale-i Nur* has been diffused in a fashion unparalleled by any other work; six hundred thousand copies have been distributed mostly in handwritten form, and have been read with the greatest ardor, both at home and abroad. What is the secret of this, and what is the reason for it?''

To questions such as this, we reply as follows: The *Risale-i Nur*, which is a true commentary upon the All-Wise Qur'an, through the property of its miraculousness, shows that misguidance is a species of Hell already in this world, and that guidance is a form of Paradise already in this world. It shows the painful torments contained within sin, evil and forbidden pleasures, and establishes that there are fine pleasures to be discovered within good deeds, fine qualities and acting according to the truths of God's Law, pleasures akin to those of Paradise. It is thus able to save the sensible among the people of vice and misguidance. For in this age there are two awesome states.

The first: since man's senses, that fail to see the ultimate outcome of things and prefer an ounce of immediate pleasure to tons of future pleasure, habitually gain dominance over intelligence and thought, the only way to deliver the people of vice from their vice is to show to them the pain inherent in their pleasure and thus to vanquish the senses. As the verse

"they deem lovable the life of this world[19]"

indicates, the only path of deliverance from the danger of preferring the fragile fragments of glass of this world to the diamondlike bounties and pleasures of the hereafter, and following the

19. Qur'an 14:3

people of misguidance in their love of the world, even while being a believer oneself, is to show the hellish torment and pain present already in this world. This is precisely the method used by the *Risale-i Nur*.

In the face of the obstinacy that arises from the intoxication produced by the misguidance and vice that arise in turn from the absolute unbelief and science prevalent in this age, only one in ten or twenty may profit from the method that consists of speaking of God Almighty, proving the existence of Hell and attempting to dissuade men from evil and vice by means of its torment. For having heard the lesson, he may say, "God is forgiving and merciful, and hell is far off," and then continue with his vice. His heart and spirit will have been conquered by his senses.

Now most of the comparisons contained in the *Risale-i Nur* show the painful and terrifying consequences in this world of unbelief and misguidance; thus they inspire in the most obstinate and lustful of men disgust at illicit and inauspicious pleasures and vices, and induce the sensible among them to make repentance.

The small comparisons contained in the Sixth, Seventh, and Eighth Words, as well as the long comparison in the Third Stopping-Place of the Thirty-Second Word, terrify even the most vicious of the misguided, and veritably impose their lesson upon him.

For example, we shall indicate very briefly the circumstances seen as truth on the imaginary journey contained in the Light Verse. Those who desire the details should refer to pages 246 to 248 of the *Coin of the Unseen*.

When I saw the animal realm, needy of sustenance, on my imaginary journey, I looked upon it with the eye of materialist philosophy. It showed that realm to me to be extremely painfull and full of torment, on account of extreme need and hunger, as well as weakness and powerlessness. I cried out in pain, for I had looked upon it with the eye of the people of misguidance and neglect.

Then I looked through the telescope of Qur'anic wisdom and faith and saw the name of Compassionate rising like a bright sun in the sign of Provider. It gilded the wretched and hungry world of the animate with the light of its mercy.

I saw then, within the animal realm, another world where young creatures were trembling on account of weakness, powerlessness and need, in a sad and painful darkness enough to inspire pity in anyone. But then I said, "Alas! again I have been looking with the gaze of the misguided." Suddenly faith gave me a pair of spectacles and I saw the name of Merciful rising in the sign of solicitude. It transformed that painful abode into a world of joy and illumined it in so fine and pleasing a fashion that the tears that had been shed in lamentation, pity and sorrow were turned into tears of joy and gratitude for pleasures enjoyed.

Then the world of man appeared before me like a cinema screen. I looked at it through the telescope of the people of misguidance, and I saw that world to be so dark and awesome that I cried out from the depths of my heart. For men were living an extremely brief and troubled life, anxious every day and every hour about the coming of death, despite their desires and hopes extending to eternity, their imaginings and thoughts embracing the whole cosmos, their aspirations and innate dispositions desiring most seriously eternal life, eternal felicity and Paradise, their unlimited and unfettered innate powers, their needs directed to innumerable purposes, and the innumerable enemies and disasters to whose attacks they are exposed. They were, moreover, suffering the constant misfortune of decline and separation, a misfortune that is most painful and awesome for their hearts and their consciences, and looking toward the tomb and the graveyard that appear for the people of neglect to be the gate to eternal darkness. I saw all men, singly and in groups, being cast into that pit of darkness.

When I saw the world of men in this darkness, all of my human capacities, including my heart, my spirit, and my intelligence, together with all the particles of my body, became ready to weep and lament. Suddenly a light and strength coming from the Qur'an broke those spectacles of misguidance and gave me a light whereby I saw God Almighty's name of Just rising in the sign of All-Wise, the name of Compassionate rising in the sign of Generous, the name of Merciful rising in the sign of Forgiving, the name of Resurrector rising in the sign of Inheritor, the name of Quickener rising in the sign of Beneficent, and the name of Lord rising in the sign of Monarch, each like a sun (by "sign" here, "meaning" is to be understood). They suddenly illumined and rejoiced the whole dark realm of humanity, together with the further realms it contained within itself. Dispersing all traces of hellish circumstance, they opened windows onto the luminous realm of the hereafter, and scattered light over the distraught world of men. I said, "praise be to God and thanks be to God, to the number of particles in the cosmos." And I saw and knew with utter certainty that even in this world there is a form of paradise contained in belief and a form of hell contained in misguidance.

Then the world of the globe displayed itself to me. On my imaginary journey, the dark scientific powers of a philosophy disobedient to religion presented to my imagination a frightening world. The state of the wretched human species that was travelling through the infinite void of the cosmos on a terrifying ship — namely the ancient globe, full of internal revolutions and earthquakes, traversing a distance of twenty-five thousand years* in a single year with a speed seventy times faster than that of a cannonball and being ever ready to disintegrate — that state appeared to me to be one of terrifying darkness. I cast the spectacles of philosophy to the ground and broke them. Suddenly I looked with an eye illumined by the wisdom of the Qur'an. I saw that various names of the Creator of the Heavens and Earth, such as All-Powerful, All-Knowing, Lord, God, Lord of the Heavens and Earth,

*i.e., twenty-five thousand years' walking distance.

and Subjugator of the Sun and Moon, were rising like suns in the signs of Mercy, Magnificence and Dominicality. They illumined the dark, awesome and terrifying world in such manner that with my believing eye I saw the globe to be like a well-ordered and equipped, a pleasant and safe cruiser, stocked up with food and provision for everyone and prepared for pleasure, recreation and trade; I saw it to be like a ship, a plane, a train destined to travel in the dominical realm around the sun of animate beings and bring to all that required sustenance the fruits of the summer, spring and fall. I said, "Praise be to God to the number of particles of the globe."

In numerous other comparisons of this kind throughout the *Risale-i Nur*, it has been proven that the people of vice and misguidance suffer even in this world a form of the torment of hell. And the people of belief and righteousness, while still in this world, are able to taste the pleasures of a form of paradise, with the stomach given them by Islam and true humanity, the manifestations of faith. They benefit, indeed, in accordance with their degree of faith.

But in this tempestuous age, the currents that deaden our senses, and disperse our gazes to the farthest horizons while yet stifling them, have induced in men a state of bewilderment akin to the numbing of senses, so that the people of misguidance cannot for the moment fully feel the torment they are suffering. The people of guidance are also afflicted by neglect and cannot fully appreciate the pleasures they are tasting.

The second awesome state in this age: in former times, the rebelliousness that arose from the misguidance and obstinacy proceeding from utter unbelief and science was slight, compared with the present age. For that reason, the lessons and proofs offered by the classical scholars of Islam were quite adequate. Unbelief arising from doubt they swiftly removed. Since belief in God was general, through making mention of God and warning of the torment of hellfire, they were able to make most men desist from vice and misguidance.

But now, whereas before only one absolute unbeliever could be found in a whole country, a hundred can be found in a single small town. It has become a hundred times more common for someone to be misguided on account of science and to rebel against the verities of faith.

Since these obstinate rebels oppose the truths of faith with an arrogance approaching that of the Pharaoh and with a most awesome kind of misguidance, a sacred truth is needed to confront them that will explode like an atomic bomb and destroy their foundations in this world. Only then will their aggression be halted and a group of them be brought to believe.

Thanks without limit be then to God Almighty that the *Risale-i Nur*, a perfect cure for the wounds of the age, a miracle and a flash proceeding from the Qur'an of Miraculous Exposition, breaks numerous obstinate rebels with its numerous comparisons, thanks to the cutting sword of the Qur'an. The proofs and arguments it adduces for the divine unity and the truths of faith, as numerous as the particles of the cosmos, show that it has never been defeated by the attacks mounted against it for twenty-five years; on the contrary, it has triumphed and continues to do so.

The *Risale-i Nur* proves visibly the comparisons it makes between belief and unbelief, between guidance and misguidance, and all the truths of belief.

For example, if all the comparisons are seen to be like the proofs of the two stations of the Twenty-Second Word, the First Stopping-Place of the Thirty-Second Word, and the Windows of the Thirty-Third Word, and if careful attention is paid, it will be understood that that which is destined to break and shatter the absolute unbelief and rebellious, obstinate misguidance of the present age, is the Qur'anic Truth manifest in the *Risale-i Nur*.

God willing, just as the important talismans of religion and the sections uncovering the riddles of the creation of the world have been gathered together in "The Collection of Talismans," so too the sections of the *Risale-i Nur* that show the people of misguidance to have their own hell in this world, and the people of guidance to taste the pleasures of paradise in this world, that show belief to be the seed out of which Paradise grows, and unbelief to be the seed from which grows the noisome tree of Hell — these sections also will be gathered together in a small collection and published.

The Seed of Paradise

(The four points of the First Topic of the Twenty-Third Word, a proof of the fact that the seed of Paradise is found in faith in this world.)

In the Name of God, the Compassionate, the Merciful, "Verily We have created man in the fairest of forms, then sent him down to the lowest of the low, except those who believe and do good deeds.[20]"

FIRST TOPIC

We shall set forth only five among the thousands of virtues of faith, this in five points.*

First point: Man rises to the highest of the high by virtue of the light of faith, and gains a value worthy of Paradise. It is by virtue of the darkness of unbelief that he falls to the lowest of the low, and enters a state deserving of hell. For faith relates man to his Glorious Maker, faith being a form of relationship. Therefore man gains value with respect to the divine artistry and the impress of the dominical names that appear in him through faith.

Unbelief severs that relationship, and as a result of this severance dominical artistry becomes

20. Qur'an 95:4-6
*Only the four relevant to the subject are included here.

hidden, so that man's value becomes restricted to the matter of which he is composed. Now matter has only an ephemeral, vanishing, impermanent and animal life; hence its value is next to nothing.

Let us expound this mystery with a metaphor. In the case of human arts, the value of the art is quite separate from the value of the material used. The two values are sometimes equal; sometimes the material is more valuable; and sometimes a five-dollar work of art may use a scrap of iron worth five cents. Sometimes, indeed, an antique may be worth millions, even though the material out of which it is made is worth not even five cents. If such an antique is taken to the antique dealer's market and attributed to some wonder craftsman or ancient and accomplished artist, that artist being recalled and commemorated, the antique will be sold for a million. But if it be taken to the scrap metal dealers, it will be sold for five cents as an old fragment of iron.

Man too is an antique work of art produced by God. He is a delicate and subtle miracle of God's power, which created man as a field for the manifestation of all the names and a miniature specimen of the whole cosmos.

If the light of faith enters his inner being, all the meaningful signs and imprints he bears will be read in that light. The believer will himself read the signs with awareness and cause others to read them. The dominical artistry inherent in man will proclaim itself with such meanings as "I am the product and creature of the Glorious Maker, the manifestation of His mercy and generosity.''

In other words, faith which consists of relationship with the Creator makes apparent all the traces of His artistry in man. The value of man is derived from that dominical artistry, that mirror of Eternal Besoughtedness. Man, without significance in himself, thus becomes superior to all of creation, the object of God's address and a dominical traveller worthy of Paradise.

But if unbelief — the severance of relationship — enters the inner being of man, then all the profound imprints of the divine names will recede into the darkness and become illegible. For if the Maker be forgotten, those spiritual aspects that are oriented to him will also be forgotten and, as it were, be cast down. Most of those profound and exalted arts, those meaningful and exalted designs, will become hidden. As for the remainder, the part visible to the eye, being attributed to causes, nature and accident, they will ultimately fall silent. Whereas each was once a brilliant diamond, each becomes now a dull piece of glass. Their only significance will be with respect to animal matter. As for the fruit and purpose of matter, it is, as we have said, to spend a brief life as the most powerless, needy and grieving among all the animals, before dissolving and departing. It is thus that unbelief destroys the essence of man, and transforms diamonds into coal.

Second point: faith, being a light, illumines man and renders legible all the letters of the Eternally Besought One that are inscribed upon him. It illumines also the whole cosmos, delivering past and future from the darkness. Let us set forth a metaphor recording a vision indicating that the verse,

"God is the protector of the believers; He brings them forth from darkness into light,[21]"

refers to this mystery.

In an imaginary vision, I saw two high mountains facing each other and joined by an awe-inspiring bridge. Beneath the bridge, on which I found myself standing, there was a deep valley. A dense gloom and darkness had submerged the whole world. I looked to my right and saw or imagined a vast grave in the midst of the darkness. I looked to my left, and it was as if I saw huge tempests, apocalypses and misfortunes being prepared in the waves of the gloom. I looked underneath the bridge, and thought that I saw a most deep precipice. Against all this darkness, my only resource was a feeble pocket lamp. I switched it on, and looking in its flickering light, beheld a most awesome sight. In front of me on the bridge there came into view terrifying dragons, lions and ravening beasts. I wished to myself that I had not had the pocket lamp in order to be able to see them. In whatever direction I turned my lamp, I received similar frights.

So I said, "this lamp is a misfortune for me," and angered at it, cast it on the ground so that it broke. As the lamp broke, it was as if I had

21. Qur'an 2:257

touched the switch of a vast electric lamp that illumined the world, for suddenly the darkness was dispersed and everywhere was filled with the light of the lamp. The reality of all things became apparent. I looked and saw that the bridge I had seen was a highway leading across a level plain. The vast grave I had seen on my right I now realized to be an assembly of worship, service, companionship and invocation, gathered in verdant gardens under the direction of luminous men. As for the tempestuous abysses I had imagined to be on my left, I saw them to be a magnificent banqueting place, a pleasant promenade, an exalted place of recreation, situated behind adorned, pleasant and attractive mountains.

And as for the creatures I had thought to be awesome beasts, and dragons, I now saw them to be tame animals such as camels, oxen, sheep, and goats.

Saying, "praise be to God for the light of faith," I recited the verse,

> "God is the protector of those who believe;
> He brings them forth from darkness into
> light.[22]"

Now those two mountains were the beginning and the end of life, the world of the earth and the world of the intermediate realm. The bridge was the road of life. My right hand was the past, and my left hand, the future.

The pocket lamp was human egoism, that is

22. Qur'an 2:257

conceited, relies on its own knowledge, and refuses to listen to heavenly revelation. The things I had imagined to be wild beasts were the vicissitudes of this world and its strange creatures.

Now the man who trusts his own egoism, who falls into the darkness of neglect, who is afflicted by the darkness of misguidance, resembles my first state in that vision. For with his deficient and misguidance-polluted knowledge, he sees the past to be a vast grave in the midst of the darkness of the void, and the future to be a place of terror, tempestuous and delivered over entirely to fate. He also regards the vicissitudes and creatures of this world as wild beasts, even though they are in reality obedient servants of One Wise and Merciful. He thus furnishes an illustration of the verse,

> "those who disbelieve, their protectors are the tyrants; they bring them forth from light into darkness.[23]"

But if man receives divine guidance, if faith enters his heart, if the tyranny of his soul is broken, if he heeds the Book of God, then he will come to resemble my second state in the vision. Then the whole of the cosmos will assume the color of daylight and be filled with divine light. The whole world will recite the verse,

> "God is the light of the heavens and the earth.[24]"

23. Qur'an 2:257
24. Qur'an 24:35

Then, with his heart's eye, he will see past time no longer as a vast grave, but rather as the passage of each age, under the direction of a prophet or a saint, to high station after the hosts of pure spirits have fulfilled their life's task of worship.

Looking to his left, he will perceive in the distance, through his light of faith, a feast of the Compassionate One set up in the pavilions of joy of Paradise that lie behind the mountains of change and vicissitude in the intermediate realm and the hereafter. He will recognize tempest and earthquake to be no more than submissive servants. Phenomena such as spring storms and rainfall, he will see to be the source of most delicate wisdom, despite their outward harshness of appearance. He will see death to be the preface to eternal life and the grave, the gateway to eternal happiness. Deduce the sense of the remaining aspects of the metaphor from what has already been said.

Third point: faith is both light and strength. Whoever acquires true faith can throw down a challenge to the whole cosmos. Depending on the strength of his faith, he can be delivered from the pressure of accident and vicissitude. Saying, "I place my trust in God," he passes through the mountainous waves of vicissitudes in utmost security, aboard the ship of life. He entrusts to the powerful hand of the One Possessing Absolute Power all of his difficulties, and tranquilly passes through the world, taking his rest in the intermediate realm. Then he flies to Paradise in order to enter everlasting felicity.

But if he does not place his trust in God, the difficulties of this world will not cause him to fly, but on the contrary, drag him down to the lowest of the low. In other words: faith brings about assertion of the divine unity, that assertion brings about submission, submission brings about trust, and trust brings about happiness in both worlds.

However, do not misunderstand! The placing of trust in God does not mean a total rejection of causes. It consists rather of regarding causes as a veil behind which the hand of God's power is at work; of considering recourse to causes as a form of active prayer; of seeking the effects of those causes only from God; of knowing all results to proceed from Him; and of being grateful to Him.

The state of the one who places his trust in God and the one who does not will be apparent from the following story.

Once two men, heavily laden with baggage, bought their tickets and boarded a ship. One of them put down his baggage as soon as they boarded, and sitting on it began to keep watch. The other man, an arrogant fool, refused to put his baggage down. He was told, "put your baggage down and be comfortable." But he replied, "no, I won't put it down; it might get lost. I am strong enough to hold my luggage in my arms and to carry it on my head."

So then they said to him: "This safe royal ship that carries both us and you is much stronger than you are, and better able to protect your baggage. You might become giddy, and fall with your baggage into the ocean. You will certainly become weaker as time passes. Your stooping back and empty head will become unable to bear the increasing weight of your baggage. And if the captain sees you in this state, he will have you thrown off the ship as a madman, or order you imprisoned as a slanderer mocking him and his ship. In either case you will be the laughing stock of people. For you have made yourself ridiculous with your arrogance that in the eyes of the perceptive shows only your weakness, and your pretentiousness that shows only hypocrisy and vileness. Everyone is laughing at you!"

Upon hearing this, the wretch came to his senses. He put his baggage down and sat on it.

"May God reward you!" he said. "I have been delivered from trouble, imprisonment and ridicule."

So O man without trust in God! You too should come to your senses and place your trust in God. Only then will you be delivered from beggary from all the cosmos, quivering in the face of every vicissitude, from selling your own soul, from ridicule, and from the imprisonment of eternal wretchedness and the pressure of this world.

Fourth point: it is faith that makes man a man; rather it makes man a monarch. This being the case, the fundamental duty of man is faith and prayer. As for unbelief, it turns man into a powerless wild beast.

Among the thousands of proofs for this statement, the differences between the ways in which men and animals come into the world constitute sufficient proof, and a decisive argument.

Yes, the differences in the ways in which men and animals come into the world show that it is faith that makes man truly man. For when an animal comes into the world, it is as if it had already been developed to perfection in another world, for it is sent here perfectly developed, in accordance with its own capacities. In the space of two hours, two days or two months, it learns all the conditions of its own life, the nature of its relations with other beings and the laws of its existence, acquiring this knowledge with the utmost firmness. An animal such as a sparrow or a bee can acquire, by way of inspiration, in a mere twenty days, the power of life and activity that man gains only in twenty years. It follows that the fundamental duty of animals is not gradually to attain perfection by means of instruction, to advance by means of the acquisition of knowledge, to seek aid and pray for succor by demonstrating powerlessness. Their duty is rather to act and worship God by their actions, in accordance with their capacities.

As for man, when he comes to the world, he needs to learn everything and is ignorant of the laws of life. He cannot learn the conditions of his life even in twenty years. In fact he needs to continue learning to the end of his life. He is sent to the world extremely weak and powerless; it takes him one or two years even to be able to stand on his own feet. He can barely distinguish between what is harmful and what is beneficial by the time he is fifteen. Through the assistance he receives from his human environment, he becomes barely able to attract benefit and to repel harm.

The inherent function of man is therefore to advance to perfection by means of instruction, to worship God by means of prayer and supplication.

He must know by whose mercy he is so wisely administered; by whose generosity he is so tenderly nurtured; and with what favor he is so delicately reared. It is further the function and duty of man to supplicate God, the Fulfiller of All Need, with the tongue of weakness and poverty, for those numerous needs not one of which his own hand can attain. In other words, it is the function of man to fly on the wings of weakness and poverty to the lofty station of worship and bondsmanship.

Man came to this world to attain perfection by means of knowledge and supplication. With respect to its quiddity and capacity, everything is connected with knowledge. The foundation, source, light and spirit of all knowledge is the knowledge of God, and the fundament of the knowledge of God is belief in God.

Since man is exposed to innumerable misfortunes despite his infinite weakness; subject to the attacks of innumerable enemies; afflicted by innumerable needs despite his infinite poverty; and needy of innumerable objects, his fundamental and inherent duty and function is, after belief, prayer and supplication. Prayer is the very fundament of worship and bondsmanship.

In order to attain some desire or wish that lies beyond his reach, a child will either weep or ask for it. That is, he will engage in a form of supplication, either in deed or in word, with the tongue of powerlessness, and thus reach his desired goal. So too man is like a delicate and spoiled child in this world of the animate. It is necessary for him either to weep in weakness and impotence or to supplicate in poverty and neediness at the threshold of the Compassionate and Merciful One. Thus his aims will be made submissive to him and he will offer thanks for their submission. Otherwise like a foolish child troubled by a fly, he will say, "with my own strength, I will subdue this apparently invincible object and wondrous objects a thousand times stronger than it. With my reflection and stratagems, I will make it obedient to myself." Thus he will stray into ingratitude for favors received, and make himself worthy of a severe chastisement.

★ ★ ★

A Comparison

WHEN THE SPOKESMAN for the people of misguidance is unable to find any support or basis on which to build his misguidance and is thus defeated in argument, he will say the following:

"Since I regard worldly felicity, the pleasure of life, the progress of civilization and the perfection of arts as all lying in refusal to think of the hereafter and to know God, in love of this world, in absolute freedom and licence and in relying exclusively on myself, I have drawn most men onto this path, through the assistance of Satan, and continue to do so."

The answer to this: We say, in the name of the Qur'an: O wretched man! Come to your senses! Do not listen to the spokesman for the people of misguidance. If you do listen to him, your loss will be so great that your spirit, intelligence and heart will shudder even to imagine it. There are two paths in front of you.

The first: the path of wretchedness laid out in front of you by the spokesman for the people of misguidance.

The second: the path of happiness defined for

167

you by the All-Wise Qur'an.

You will have noted and understood numerous comparisons between these two paths in the Words, particularly the Short Words. Note and understand now one of the thousands of comparisons, suitable to our present discussion:

The path of assigning partners to God, misguidance, lechery and vice, causes man to fall to the lowest degree. Afflicted with infinite pains, he is caused to take up an infinitely heavy burden and fasten it to his weak and powerless waist. For if man does not recognize God and place his trust in Him, he will become extremely weak and impotent, extremely needy and impoverished, a suffering, grieving and ephemeral animal, exposed to infinite misfortunes. Suffering continuously the pain of separation from all the objects of love and attachment, he will ultimately abandon all of his loved ones and go alone to the darkness of the grave.

Throughout his life, he struggles vainly, with an extremely slight will, restricted power, a short lifespan and a dull imagination, against infinite pains and hopes. To no avail, he strives to attain innumerable desires and goals.

Even though he is unable to bear his own burden, he loads the vast world onto his wretched waist and brain. He suffers the torment of Hell before even arriving there.

Yes, in order to avoid feeling this disquieting pain, this awesome spiritual torment, the people of misguidance have recourse to a drunkenness that is like a form of stupor and they are temporarily able to avoid feeling their pain. But when they do feel it, they suddenly feel the proximity of the grave. For whoever is not a true bondsman of God will imagine himself to be his own master. But with his partial and limited will and his petty power and strength, he is unable to administer and control this tempestuous world. He sees attacking him thousands of different species of enemy, from harmful microbes to earthquakes. In an awesome state of painful fear, he looks toward the gate of the tomb, that at all times appears dreadful to him.

While in this state, man will also be troubled by the state of the world and of man, for as a human being he is attached to the human species and to the world, but he does not imagine the world and man to be in the control of One All-Wise, All-Knowing, All-Powerful, Merciful and Generous, and has attributed them instead to chance and to nature. Together with his own pains, he suffers also the pains of the world. Earthquakes, plagues, storms, famine and scarcity, separation and decease — all of this torments him in the most painful and sombre fashion.

But the man who finds himself in this state is not worthy of pity and sympathy, for he is himself responsible for it.

As was said in the Eighth Word, in the comparison between two brothers who entered the well, one who is not content with a refreshing, sweet, honorable, pleasant and licit drink, consumed in a pleasant garden, at a pleasant gathering of pleasant friends, and then, drinking some ugly and unclean wine for the sake of illicit and impure pleasure, imagines himself in some foul place in the middle of winter, surrounded by wild animals — such a one is not worthy of pity, for he imagines his honorable and blessed companions to be wild beasts, and thus insults them.

He will further imagine the delicious foods and clean dishes at the gathering to be impure and filthy stones, and will therefore begin breaking them. He will imagine the respected books and profound writings circulating at the gathering to be meaningless and banal designs, will tear them and cast them underfoot. Such a person is not merely unworthy of mercy, he also deserves beating.

So too the one who through the intoxication of unbelief, arising from incorrect choice, and the lunacy of misguidance, imagines this hospice of the world of the All-Wise Maker to be the plaything of chance and natural forces; who fancies that the passage into the world of the unseen of those creatures that constantly renew the manifestation of the divine names, after the completion of their duties with the passage of time, is execution and annihilation; who thinks that the echoes of glorification of God, heard throughout the cosmos, are the lamentations of death and eternal separation; who deems the pages of created beings — those inscriptions of the Eternally Besought One — to be meaningless and confused; who imagines the gate of the tomb, that opens onto the world of mercy, to be the mouth of the darkness of annihilation; who deems the appointed hour, which is in reality an invitation to join his true friends, the herald of separation from all his friends — such a person denies, denigrates and insults creation, God's Names and Inscriptions, and is therefore not only unworthy of compassion and sympathy but also deserving of severe torment. He is not in any way worthy of mercy.

O wretched people of misguidance and vice! What accomplishment of yours, what art, what perfection, what civilization, what progress, can confront this awesome silence of the grave, this painful despair? Where can you find that true consolation that is the most urgent need of the human spirit?

What natural causes — in which you place so much trust and to which you attribute the works of God and the bounties of the Lord — what causality, what partner attributed by you to God, what discovery, what nationality, what false object of worship, can deliver you from the darkness of death that you imagine to be eternal annihilation, and enable you to cross the frontiers of the grave, the boundaries of the intermediate realm, the marches of the plain of resurrection, the Bridge of Sirat? Which of these things can bring about your eternal felicity? But know that you will of a certainty travel on this path, for you cannot close the gate of the tomb. A traveller on such a path ought of a certainty to put his trust in one whose control and command embraces all this vast sphere and its extensive boundaries.

O wretched people of misguidance and neglect! In accordance with the principle that "the consequence of an illicit love is suffering a merciless torment," you are suffering a fully justified punishment, for you are employing your innate capacity for love and knowledge, the ability to give thanks and worship, that relate properly to the Essence, Attributes and Names of God Almighty, on your own soul and the life of this world, in illicit fashion. For you will have lavished the love that belongs to God Almighty on your own soul, and you will suffer the infinite torment of the soul, your object of love. For you will not be bestowing true tranquility on your soul, insofar as you are failing to deliver it trustingly to the Possessor of Absolute Power Who is the only true object of love.

You suffer a further misfortune through bestowing on the world the love that properly pertains to the names and attributes of God and dividing His works among the secondary causes of the world. For one group of those innumerable beloveds of yours will turn their backs on you and leave you without even saying goodbye. Another group will not even recognize you, or if they do, they will not love you. Or if they love you, their love will be of no use. You will constantly suffer from innumerable separations and farewells without hope of return.

This, then, is the true nature and essence of what the people of misguidance call the source of life's happiness, human perfection, advanced civilization and the pleasure of freedom. Vice

and intoxication are but a veil, and make it possible to stop feeling temporarily. Say then, "I
spit on the intelligence of those who follow such
a path!"

But as for the luminous highway of the Qur'an,
it cures with the verities of faith all the wounds
of the people of misguidance. It disperses all the
gloom and darkness of their path. It closes the
door on all misguidance and perdition.

Thus it cures the weakness, powerlessness,
poverty and neediness of man with trust in One
Merciful and All-Powerful. Entrusting the burden
of life and existence to His power and mercy
instead of loading it onto himself, he finds a
station of ease as if he were being carried on his
own life and soul. The Qur'an makes it known
that man is not a "rational animal," but rather a
true man, a well-accepted guest of the Compassionate One. Showing the world to be a hospice
of the Compassionate One, the beings contained
in it to be mirrors to the Divine Names, and the
created objects found in it to be the ever-fresh
inscriptions of the Eternally Besought One, it
gently cures man of the wounds inflicted on him
by the transience of the world, the ephemeral
nature of things, and the love of the insubstantial,
and delivers him from the darkness of fancy
and imagination.

It shows death and the appointed hour to be the
prelude to joining and meeting beloved ones
already in the world of eternity, and the bridge
to the intermediate realm. It thus cures the
wounds inflicted by the notion of death as eternal

separation from all friends, as held by the people of misguidance. It demonstrates that that supposed separation is in fact the truest form of meeting.

Further, by establishing that the grave is a gate opening onto the world of mercy, the abode of felicity, the garden of paradise, the luminous realm of the Compassionate One, it erases the most awesome fear in man's breast, and shows that the apparently painful, troublesome and unpleasant journey to the intermediate realm is in fact the most pleasurable, enjoyable and joyous of journeys. With the grave, it closes the mouth of the dragon, and opens a gate onto a pleasant garden. In other words, it shows the grave to be not the mouth of a dragon but a gate opening onto a garden of mercy.

The path of the Qur'an also says to the believer: "Since your will is only partial and restricted, consign your affair to the universal will of your Master! Since your power is but feeble, place your trust in the Possessor of Absolute Power! Since your life is brief, think on your eternal life! Since your lifespan is short, know that an eternal life awaits you, and do not fret! If your thoughts are dull, enter the range of the Qur'an's rays! Look with the light of faith, and each verse of the Qur'an will illumine you like a star, instead of the moth of your own mind!

"Since you have innumerable hopes and endless pains, know that infinite reward and mercy beyond limit await you. Since you have innumerable desires and wishes, do not think on them and become disturbed. This world cannot contain them;

the proper place for them is another realm, and the one who will grant them is one other than yourself.''

The path of the Qur'an also says: ''O man! You are not your own master. Rather you are the servant of a Possessor of Infinite Power, unbounded Mercy and Absolute Glory. Do not therefore trouble yourself with the burden of your own life; for it is He Who grants your life and disposes of it.

''The world has also not been left to its own devices, so that you need to trouble yourself with the burden of concern for the state of the world, for the Master of this world is all-wise, all-knowing. You are a guest here; do not meddle in the affairs of your host!

''Creatures such as men and animals have also not been left to their own devices; rather each of them has been entrusted with a duty, and is watched over by One Wise and Merciful. Do not concern yourself with their pains and afflictions, thus causing pain to yourself. Do not try to be more tender and compassionate than their Merciful Creator. The threads of all those things that are hostile to you — microbes, plagues, storms, famine and earthquakes — are in the hands of that Merciful and Wise One. Being wise, He does nothing hazardously; being merciful, His mercy is superabundant, and a form of grace and favor is contained in each of His deeds.''

The path of the Qur'an also says: ''This world is indeed ephemeral; it produces, however, the instruments needed for an eternal world. It is transient and passing, but it yields eternal fruits, and displays the manifestations of the eternal names of an eternal Being. Its pleasures are indeed few and its pains plentiful, but the favors of the Compassionate and Merciful One are everlasting and true pleasures. As for the pains of this world, they too ultimately lead to pleasure because of the reward to be had for enduring them.

"Since the sphere of the licit is sufficient for all the pleasures, delights and joys of the spirit, heart and soul, do not enter the sphere of the illicit. For one pleasure within that sphere sometimes entails one thousand pains, apart from causing the loss of those favors of the Compassionate One that are true and lasting pleasure.

"Moreover, the path of misguidance, as set forth above, causes man to descend to the lowest of the low in such manner that no philosophy, no civilization can furnish a remedy, and no amount of human progress or technical accomplishment can deliver him. By contrast, the All-Wise Qur'an elevates man, through belief and good deeds, from the lowest of the low to the highest of the high. It fills in that deep pit with the rungs of spiritual progress and inner advancement.

"It facilitates also man's long, stormy and troublesome journey into eternity. It displays to him means for traversing a distance of a thousand, or fifty thousand, years in a single day.

"Through making known the Possessor of Glory Who is the Monarch of Pre- and Post-Eternity, it bestows on man the position of a bondsman and servant entrusted with a certain task. It makes it possible for him to journey with the utmost tranquillity both in the hospice of this world and also in the stages and stopping places of the intermediate world and the realm of the hereafter.

"The direct appointee and servant of a monarch will travel through his realm with ease and by the fastest means possible, such as airplane, ship or train. So too the one who establishes a relation with the Pre-Eternal Monarch by means of good deeds and belief will pass with the speed of lightning or of Buraq (the Prophet's mount during his Ascension) through the stages of this hospice of the world, the spheres of the intermediate realm and the world of resurrection, and the frontiers of all the realms that lie beyond the grave, thus attaining eternal felicity. The Qur'an establishes this truth in decisive fashion, and shows it to the pure and saintly ones."

The truth of the Qur'an also says: "O believer! Do not give your infinite capacity for love to your ugly, defective, evil and harmful instinctual soul. Do not take the soul as your object of love, nor its caprices as your object of worship. Take rather as your object of love and worship One Who is worthy of your infinite capacity of love; Who has bestowed infinite gifts upon you; Who in the future too will make you infinitely happy; Who makes happy all of those beings to whom you are attached and whose happiness is the source of your happiness; Who possesses infinite perfection and a beauty that is infinitely sacred,

exalted, transcendent, faultless, flawless and un-
fading; the beauty of Whose mercy and the mercy
of Whose beauty is demonstrated by all the
beauties and bounties of Paradise; in each of
Whose names are inherent abundant lights of
fairness and beauty; Whose beauty and perfection
are indicated by all the fairness, beauty and
virtue of all lovable and loved objects in the
cosmos.''

The Qur'an also says: "O man! Do not
wastefully squander on transient beings your
capacity to love, which properly belongs to His
names and attributes. For the works and creatures
of God are ephemeral, but the Beautiful Names
that are manifest and inscribed in them are eternal
and permanent. In each of the names and attributes there are thousands of degrees of bounty
and beauty, thousands of levels of perfection and
love. Look simply at the name of Compassionate:
Paradise is a manifestation of it, eternal felicity
is a flash deriving from it, and all the provision
and bounty in the world is a mere drop taken
from it.''

Pay attention to this verse which indicates
the essence of the people of misguidance and
that of the people of belief, as well as their respective functions:

> "verily We have created man in the fairest
> of shapes, then sent him down to the lowest
> of the low, except for those who believe
> and do good deeds.[25]"

25. Qur'an 95:4-6

Heed too this verse that indicates their final result and outcome:

"The heavens and the earth wept not over them.[26]"

In how exalted and miraculous a fashion they set forth the comparison that we have made!

Since the meaning expressed miraculously and concisely in the first verse is set out in detail in the Eleventh Word, we refer our readers to that part of the *Risale-i Nur* for a discussion of it.

As for the second verse, we will show, through a brief indication, how exalted a meaning it expresses.

The explicit meaning of the verse is that the heavens and the earth do not weep when the people of misguidance die. The implied meaning is that the heavens and the earth do weep when the people of belief depart from the world. For the people of misguidance, through their denial of the functions of the heavens and earth, their ignorance of their meaning, their rejection of their value, their refusal to recognize their Maker, are in fact acting with hostility and disrespect toward them. Naturally, then, the heavens and earth will not weep over them, but in fact curse them and rejoice at their death.

As for the implied meaning, that the heavens and earth weep over the death of the people of faith, this is because the people of faith know the functions of the heavens and earth, assent

26. Qur'an 44:29

to their true natures, and understand, through faith, the meanings they express, saying "how beautifully they have been made, how finely they are performing their functions!" They assign them their true worth and grant them their due respect. They love them and the names that they mirror for the sake of God Almighty. It is for this reason that the heavens and earth grieve over the death of the people of faith as if weeping.

★　★　★

EULOGY

Extract from a letter written by the late Muallim Hasan Feyzi, on the occasion of the escape from fire of copies of the Supreme Sign from a shop where they were kept during the great conflagration at Emirdag.

In His name, Be He Glorified!

THE RISALE-I NUR extinguishes every fire and conflagration. It extinguishes the fire of extravagance in men through the light of the "Treatise of Economy;" it extinguishes the fire of sickness in those wretches that twist and turn with fire and flame through the water of life and the curative properties that flow forth from the lights of the "Treatise for the Sick," that gush forth from its spring of twenty-five remedies; it puts out the awesome fire of fancy and caprice, anxiety and desire, that engulfs and shakes the heart, mind and all the members of man, through the light and grace of the "Treatise on Anxiety;" it extinguishes the fever of diseases such as hypocrisy and care for repute, pride and arrogance, through the aid and favor of the "Treatise on Sincerity;" and it destroys the fortress of egoism, selfishness, and impudence through the guidance contained in the Thirtieth Word [called "Ana" (English "I")] and the Sixth Word.

It is only the strong, powerful, far-reaching luminous, and intelligent hands of those parts of

181

the *Risale-i Nur* called "Nature" and "Atom and Substance" that can rescue from the pit of the matter and particle of nature those blind and dazed ones that are unable to emerge themselves.

As for dispersing the fire of the fear of death felt by the aged, its pains and anxieties, the consolation and succor, the remedy and electuary, the grace and light contained in the treatise of that name are fully enough; and the Treatises on the "Miraculousness of the Qur'an," "The Miracles of the Prophet Muhammed," and "Belief in the Hereafter" are each like a great pool filled with the water of life, able to extinguish the fire of the intermediate realm and to dispel its pain.

We believe that just as the vast light of this blessed work, "The Supreme Sign or the Staff of Moses" is able to extinguish the fire of all the polytheism on earth, so too it will continue its present expansion in the face of that red flame and black smoke that embrace the horizons of the world and are now threatening the world of Islam, and extinguish the sedition and fire of the terrible reds.

In short, the study of the *Risale-i Nur*, its constant spiritual grace, are enough to extinguish the fire of the instinctual soul, to kill its savage attributes, to overthrow all its destructive and fissiparous soldiery, whether outer or inner. It is indeed the duty of the *Risale-i Nur* to extinguish the fire of sedition and corruption, and for the sake of this that it was born and came into being.

We stress again, on the basis of the indication contained in the verse,

> "God will bring forth a people whom He shall love and who shall love Him,[27]"

of what cherished warriors is composed this blessed, auspicious, courageous and noble people of ours, living in this blessed homeland that is the cradle of saints and holy men, of warriors and conquerors.

In those who adopt and assimilate the *Risale-i Nur*, greed and rancor decline, oppressiveness and lust melt away. The fire of ignorance and wretchedness is extinguished. The slumber of immersion in nature decreases. The sleep of neglect comes to an end. Black, ugly and impure blood is purified. Soul and heart begin to work. Each vein becomes a channel of light. Neither love of the world nor desire for the hereafter remain. "I" and "thou" disappear. The veils that are said to be seventy thousand in number begin to lift, and the mountain of existence begins to show cracks. Sounds begin to be heard proclaiming,

> "return to thy Lord.[28]"

The way of attainment lies open; musk and ambergris lie scattered on all hands. The command

27. Qur'an 5:54
28. Qur'an 89:28

of

"enter among My bondsmen,[29]"

is followed by the reward of

"and enter My garden.[30]"

Show us, Thou who hast extinguished the fire
with His light,
Who hast invoked blessings on Thy beloved!

The *Risale-i Nur,* is in short, a tablet on which
is inscribed, "O Preserver," a page on which
is written, "what God wills," a sheet bearing
the inscription, "God bless it!", a hose of light
trained on the fire, a wise prescription for the
sufferer, an instructive mirror for whoever gazes
upon it, a seal of prophethood for the Muslims,
a deed of delivery for the criminal, a path of
guidance for the wanderer, a guarantee of safety
for the solitary, a treasure of eternity for the
antiquarian, a regret-inducing blow for the denier,
a gallows of justice for the unbeliever, a sacred
companion for the gnostic, a palace of union
for the beloved...

> *In the name of all the Students of*
> *Nur of Denizli and its environs*
>
> *Hasan Feyzi*
> *(God's mercy be upon him,*
> *always and eternally).*

29. Qur'an 89:29
30. Qur'an 89:30

The following is a defense speech by a student of the *Risale-i Nur*. More than 800 court cases concerning the work took place during the lifetime of the author and the first ten years after his demise. All of the trials proved that the *Risale-i Nur* is directed not toward worldly affairs, but rather toward the spiritual life of the people. (Ed.)

A defense speech presented to the Afyon Penal Court:

The prosecutor has made a mountain out of a molehill and presented me in the role of a diplomat and intriguer on account of my service to my master, whom I indeed accept with all pride, and to the *Risale-i Nur*. He has thus assigned me a major share in the alleged offence connected with the *Risale-i Nur.* In answer I say:

I am profoundly devoted to my master, Bediuzzaman, from the reading of whose works on religion, faith and ethics I have benefited to such a degree that I am ready unhesitatingly to sacrifice my life for his sake. This devotion is not, however, harmful to fatherland and people, nor does it have the purpose of inciting the people against the state, as claimed by the prosecution. It is rather an unshakeable devotion aimed at delivering from the annihilation of the tomb — something no one can hope to avoid — myself and those of my brothers in religion who wish to preserve their faith in this dangerous age, who want to purify their morals and be useful citizens of their countries and societies.

I am among the close associates of my master.

185

I have served him proudly. During the whole
time, I have witnessed from him nothing except
virtue. More than hundreds of thousands of copies
of the *Risale-i Nur,* as well as the hundreds of
thousands of sincere students of the *Risale-i Nur*
who have preserved their faith by reading these
copies, are witnesses to his utmost modesty.

My blessed master regards himself too as a
student of the *Risale-i Nur* and claims no more
than this.

It is easy to see this in many writings now in
your possession, especially the "Treatise on Sincerity" contained in the collection, "The Staff
of Moses." He repeatedly states in his treatises
and letters, "Eternal truths, like suns and
diamonds, cannot be based on ephemeral individuals, nor can ephemeral individuals claim
possession of those truths." How, then, can it
be permissible to speak of arrogance and boasting
on his part? For if you read all the Treatises
and Letters, justly and carefully, you too will
become unshakeably certain that this respected
scholar, the most learned of the age, is a scholar
of religion the like of whom has not been seen
for many centuries; an unparalleled savior of
faith; and a patriot more beneficial and blessed
for people and nation than a whole army, at
a time when the red sparks of Bolshevism are
beginning to glint on our horizon. My only regret
is that I did not earlier become a student of such
a work and its author, our respected master.

Respected tribunal! In order that my fellow
citizens should benefit from the *Risale-i Nur,*

a work the innumerable benefits of which I had myself experienced, I had the "Guide for Youth" printed in Eskisehir, with official permission, and the intention of performing a sacred duty toward the nation. I ask you, is it not contrary to all true justice, to treat with harshness a wretch such as myself, who deserves congratulation and appreciation and needs encouragement in his service to the *Risale-i Nur*, a true and unfailing commentary upon the Qur'an, and hence to faith itself?

I demand of your just court that you proclaim free and unobjectionable the *Risale-i Nur,* the nurture of our spirits, the cause of our salvation, the key of our eternal felicity. But if certain of the matters I have mentioned and set forth above constitute a crime in your eyes, then I submit to you that I will accept the heaviest punishment you can inflict with the most cordial contentment.

*Ceylan Caliskan, imprisoned
in the prison of Afyon (in 1947).*

Other Risale-i Nur Books of Interest

☐ **Fruits from the Tree of Light**
An anthology of writings
by Bediuzzaman Said Nursi $1.95

☐ **Nature: Cause or Effect?**
"This treatise puts naturalistic atheism to death
with no chance of reanimation, and totally wrecks
the foundation stones of atheism." $1.25

☐ **Sincerity and Brotherhood**
Two Essentials for believers. "This treatise should
be read at least once every two weeks." $1.25

☐ **Belief or Unbelief**
"Belief illuminates the universe, and takes the past
and the future out of darkness." $1.25

☐ **Biography of Bediuzzaman S. Nursi**
The life of the author of Risale-i Nur Collection
                                            $1.50

☐ **The Miracles of Muhammad**
The testimony of history — includes more than 300
divine miracles of the Prophet Muhammad (peace
be upon him) $2.75

Risale-i Nur Institute of America
P.O. Box 2192, Berkeley, California 94702, USA

Please send me the Risale-i Nur books I have
checked above. I am enclosing $_____(check or
money order). Please include the list price plus 35¢ a
copy to cover mailing costs. If you order six or more
copies of one title, no postage is necessary. (Prices are
subject to change without notice.)

Name_____

Address_____

City_____State_____Zip _____
Allow 4-6 weeks for delivery